THIS
PRECIOUS
LIFE

Buddhist Tsunami Relief and
Anti-Nuclear Activism in Post 3/11 Japan

Edited by
Jonathan S. Watts

The International Buddhist Exchange Center (IBEC)
Yokohama, Japan

International Buddhist Exchange Center (IBEC)

The Kodo Kyodan Buddhist Fellowship

38 Torigoe, Kanagawa-ku

Yokohama 221-0064

JAPAN

Tel: 81-45-432-1201 Fax: 81-45-432-8067

http://www.kodosan.or.jp/

Printed in Thailand by Parbpim Printing House

ISBN 978-616-7368-207

Printed on acid-free paper

Contents

Part III : Messages from International Buddhist Leaders on the Future of Japan

Editor's Foreword

Before the tragic triple disaster of earthquake, tsunami, and nuclear meltdown occurred on March 11, 2011, Japan was already a nation in crisis. The high growth period of the 1980s and Japan's rise to global economic power had given way to nearly two decades of economic stagnation. This was accompanied by a widespread deterioration in the quality of life—increased strains on workers at all levels and increasing personal bankruptcy; widening socio-economic gaps between rural and urban, rich and poor; community breakdown and personal alienation resulting in a chronically high rate of suicide amongst all ages—to make a short list. The Japanese Buddhist world has been in similar such crisis—marginalization of social roles and a pejorative image as "Funeral Buddhism", declining numbers of believers, and more recent moves by the state to revoke its tax-exempt privileges.

When the disasters of 3/11 struck, all these problems and more were brought into intensified focus. Japan has always coped with previous devastating earthquakes in various regions in the country—as recent as the Great Hanshin Earthquake of 1995 and the Chu-etsu Earthquake of 2004. However, the scale of devastation of the ensuing tsunami not only brought a heightened sense of trauma but also precipitated the nuclear meltdowns at the Fukushima #1 nuclear facility. This latter incident is still ongoing and has brought many of these aforementioned social issues into the forefront of social debate as yet to be answered questions: After two decades of economic stagnation, what is the economic vision for Japan in the 21st century? Can such an economic vision not entail the exploitation of people in the rural areas for their labor and their hosting of nuclear power facilities? What is the source of real happiness for the nation's citizens: modern virtues of economic growth and consumer accumulation or more traditional Japanese virtues of continuing bonds and human interconnection?

While Japanese Buddhism continues to grapple with its own issues, many positive developments can be seen from this past year. Japanese Buddhism showed in its efforts to aid tsunami victims that it is still alive and quite prepared to step back into the lives of the common people through service to them and their communities. While this marks a continuation of traditional roles, especially in Northeast Japan where Buddhist faith has remained strong, it also shows a resurgence in working for society among Buddhist priests, especially younger ones who continue to do tremendous work as individuals and with their various youth associations. On the other hand, Japanese Buddhism's slow response to the core issues of the nuclear issue has been in keeping with their many years of social conservatism. However, in the latter stages of 2011, we have seen a growing courage for Buddhists to come out on this issue—first, in encouraging people to re-embrace a Buddhist lifestyle of contentment over consumerism, and second, to challenge the economic and political system that has exploited many of its parishioners in rural regions.

In this volume, we have attempted to give a feel of the unfolding events of the year by structuring essays roughly in a chronological order. Part I opens with recollections and experiences from 3/11 and the immediate difficult days afterwards, focusing on the emergency relief work by Buddhist priests, their temples, and Buddhist based relief organizations. As the weeks and months passed, the relief work changed in character, and the latter essays in this section reflect that with stories of helping survivors deal with their experience of trauma and grief.

Part II focuses on the nuclear issue. Although this crisis unfolded in tandem with the tsunami one, the Buddhist world in particular was slow to address it in comparison to their timely work in the tsunami areas. This section begins with a wide-ranging essay by one of Japan's top development economists, Jun Nishikawa, who provides an excellent context for understanding the nuclear issue in Japan and Buddhism's connection to it. We are then introduced to the most radical Japanese Buddhists, involved in the nuclear issue long before the Fukushima incident. Then, we see the gradual awakening to the issue by mainstream Japanese Buddhism—a still ongoing awakening.

Part III is a shorter section on some of the important voices from the international Buddhist world directed to Japan during the year of crisis. They are voices of both sympathy and of challenge to Japanese Buddhists to take affirmative social leadership, not only in the healing of the nation but in guiding their people to a new society rooted in the perennial Buddhist virtues of non-harming (as non-exploitation) and personal contentment (as opposed to material avarice).

The editor would like to express his deepest gratitude firstly to the many authors and contributors to this volume who so generously offered their articles and stories. I would also like to express great thanks to our immediate circle of friends in the Japan Network of Engaged Buddhists (JNEB) (Rev. Kobo Inoue, Rev. Jin Sakai, and Rev. Yuzuki Matsushita in particular) for their assistance in translation, providing photos, and, most importantly, making connections to important people in the field who became contributors for this volume. A final debt of thanks goes to my wife, Naomi Takasawa, for her help in translation and support during this challenging year.

This volume represents the work of the International Buddhist Exchange Center's Engaged Buddhism Project to document in English for the world outside of Japan the experiences, activities, struggles, challenges, and hopes of the Japanese Buddhist world in confronting the 3/11 disasters and the larger implications of them. The International Buddhist Exchange Center (IBEC) was founded in 1966 by the 1st President of the Kodo Kyodan Buddhist Fellowship, Rev. Masazumi Shojun Okano. Its general goals are to develop modern, international perspectives on Buddhism through study and research, to create opportunities for those interested in Buddhism to learn and study further through lectures and events, and to cooperate with Buddhists inside and outside Japan on various social issues. IBEC's Engaged Buddhist Project (EBP) was created in April 2006 by Kodosan's 3rd President, Rev. Shojun Okano. The core focus of the project has been to investigate the activities of Japanese Buddhists, especially from traditional denominations, on social issues; that is the engaged Buddhist activities of Japanese Buddhists. The deeper emphasis of the research has been on grassroots activities focused on critical Japanese social issues, like suicide, poverty, problem youth, and since March 11th, 2011, emergency relief aid and nuclear activism.

Jonathan Watts
Yokohama, Japan
February 7, 2012

Jonathan Watts has been a research fellow at IBEC since its founding. He is also a research fellow at the Jodo Shu Research Institute working on Buddhist care for the dying and bereaved with Rev. Yoshiharu Tomatsu and at the Rinbutsuken Institute for Engaged Buddhism with Rev. Jin Hitoshi. He teaches contemporary Japanese Buddhism and social issues at Keio University. He also serves on the Executive Committee of the International Network of Engaged Buddhists (INEB). Living in Japan since 1993, he presently resides in Kamakura, just south of Tokyo, with his wife and daughter.

PART I

BUDDHIST SOCIAL WELFARE

Material and Psycho-Spiritual Aid Work

RTHERN JAPAN AND DISASTER AFFECTED AREAS

KEY

- MOST-AFFECTED PREFECTURES
- DISTRICTS WITH ASSESSED DAMAGE OR FLOODING *
- AFFECTED NUCLEAR POWER PLANTS
- - DISTANCE FROM FUKUSHIMA DAIICHI
- - DISTANCE FROM FUKUSHIMA DAINI
- - MAJOR ROADS
- - SECONDARY ROADS
- - RAILROADS

rce: U.S. Government
04/08/11

Sea of Japan

Aomori
Misawa Air Force Base
Misawa
Hirosaki
Hachinohe

Noshiro

IWATE

Miyako

Kamaishi

Ofunato

Sakata

MIYAGI
Ishinomaki
Sendai
50 mi (80km)

EPICENTER
MAGNITUDE 7.1
04/07/11

EPICENTER
MAGNITUDE 9.0
03/11/11

12 mi (20km)

FUKUSHIMA
Koriyama
6 mi (10km)

Nagaoka

Iwaki

Muraku

Nikko

PACIFIC OCEAN

Ueda
Kiryu
Hitachi

Takasaki

Matsumoto
Tsukuba

Yokota Air Force Base
Matsudo Narita
Choshi
Hachioji Tokyo Funabashi
Kawasaki
Atsugi
Yokosuka

Shimizu
Numazu
Tateyama

amamatsu

0   50   100 mi
0   50   100   150 km

JAPAN

A Zen Master's Witness of the Primeval Force of Nature

Shodo Harada Roshi

---

*M*any of the temples that were destroyed or affected in the earthquake and tsunami disaster in Northeast Japan were Zen temples. Not only these, but many other temples in the region, served as shelters for the victims of the disaster, and many priests tirelessly worked for both their material and spiritual support, while existing in this difficult environment themselves. The following letter by Rev. Shodo Harada gives an up-close and personal look at the situation in the area near Sendai City in Miyagi Prefecture. Rev. Harada is a Rinzai priest, author, head abbot of Sogen-ji—a three hundred year old temple in Okayama Prefecture—and dharma heir of Yamada Mumon Roshi (1990-1988), one of the great Rinzai masters of the twentieth century. His students have begun more than a dozen affiliated Zen groups, known as One Drop Zendos, in the United States, Europe, and Asia.

To all of the One Drop Zendos around the world, to the many people concerned, and to those with whom we have a karmic affiliation, I am writing to you about the recent great earthquake and tsunami tragedy. From their most profound mind, everyone has worried about us and supported the disaster relief. I deeply thank you from the bottom of my heart.

Preparation for the Journey North

In Sendai, there is a priest and a temple, Zenno-ji, with which we have strong karmic affiliation. He has always sent robes *(samugi)*, rice, and straw sandals for going on alms round for the people training at Sogen-ji. In some way, then; in any way possible, I wanted to go there and support him. The shinkansen (high speed train) was not yet running up there; the local trains were irregular and frequently nonexistent; and all the roads had been destroyed and were still impassable. Anywhere near the site of the disaster was impossible to enter, except for the national guard and other emergency groups in their special vehicles. Regular vehicles could not get there. On March 27th, the roads finally were opened, and so using every possible means we were able to go to Sendai and to the Fukushima area.

Yet there was also radiation leaking from the damaged nuclear power plants, and it was known to be a very risky situation. Considering the one chance out of a thousand in which something could go wrong, it was decided to not take younger people training at Sogen-ji there, so Ekei Zenji and Domyo Koji were taken to represent the sangha. We took all kinds of food supplies and dishes to eat at meals. They had told us on the phone that they could only make cooked rice for us and that they had nothing to eat with it. "We have no supplies or fuel, so please bring your own food," they told us. "We want to go visiting here and there, so for the children and the various evacuees, please, as much as possible, bring sweets and simple foods that they can eat without any need for preparation."

The people at Sogen-ji worked as hard as they could to get the bread baking done and get as many loaves of bread made as possible before our departure. It was very insufficient, only a little something in a time of big need, but our time had been limited. People gathered candy to bring as well. Since there is very little water available and they cannot brush their teeth, they also asked for gum that cleans your teeth when you chew it. We also packed many, many hot packs, since it was still very cold. As we didn't know what we would encounter, we went in boots, warm clothes, and *samugi*.

Temples and Priests Hard at Work

In the morning, we arrived in Sendai. There were many buildings that were still standing erect and appeared to have no damage, so there was a strange weird feeling. After our bus came into Sendai station, the priest who was supposed to pick us up arrived, and we put our packages into his car. As we drove, the priest told us that although the buildings looked normal, inside all the offices were completely turned upside down and a mess. Not one single place can still be used inside the buildings.

Zenno-ji temple is located about twenty minutes from the station. Zenno-ji had been seriously damaged. There were 1,600 graves in the cemetery and every last gravestone had toppled over. It was a hideous scene. The main hall was just barely being covered by its roof. There were continual aftershocks every thirty minutes or so. The priest said that they could not even use the main hall yet. There were big cracks in the great stone lanterns, and all of the rocks were falling around, having been loosened by the disaster. Even so the buildings were somehow still standing and had been protected even in such a severe disaster. He said that was already a great good fortune.

They already had their life lines of electricity and water reconnected from a few days before, but they were still without gas. They apologized for not being able to make a bath for us. The priest's wife came out and greeted us saying she had prepared some rice balls. Eating them with instant miso soup, we had breakfast. That day when we arrived, we were first to go around and look at the area, and take around the things we had brought. The next day, from the morning, we would work on the cleaning up of the Zenno-ji temple and house.

First, we went to Furin-ji temple, related to Zennoji's abbot's wife. Furin-ji was in the very middle of the worst hit part of the earthquake and tsunami, but the temple itself is just a bit above the worst-hit area. Mysteriously, it did not suffer any damage whatsoever. The water of the tsunami washed right up to the main gate of the temple, and just because of its being built on slightly higher ground, it was not affected by the wave. All of the houses up to main gate were completely and totally destroyed. The temple priest had welcomed 200 people to live there, and every day was making food for them. At a time like this, the extensive size of a temple grounds was put to good use. The temple was able to welcome everyone in the area, to serve them, and to protect them within the temple grounds.

The Mysterious and Awesome Power of Nature

In these areas, seeing all the various conditions, we continued to drive around in the car and came out on the other side of the hills at a place called Shirahama, at the mouth of the Matsushima Bay. There are seven small islands here. Because this area is a place famous for its great beauty, each and every small island has a temple, seven of them all together. One of them, called Dosho-ji temple, was the temple of a friend of Zenno-ji. We went there to visit next. This is the furthest small island and the water that had swept over it had destroyed its entire small town of 3,000 people, all in the one instant that the wave poured over them.

The head priest of that temple ran a kindergarten at the temple. Taking the children of the kindergarten, they had run up to the top of the mountain and been saved. But everything else just up to the top of that mountain had been swallowed up and covered in the tsunami's waters, buried. No matter how hard he looked for a path down from the top, he was not able to find one. Everything had been destroyed, and strewn everywhere. They all were eventually rescued from the top of the mountain by a national guard helicopter. One after another, they had been lifted up and rescued by the helicopter—this scene was played again and again on televisions all over Japan.

Passing hill after hill of debris we continued past the seven islands, went over the mountain, and came out at Shiogama, the next town. Here in Shiogama, there were homes that had no one had yet entered into, so they had not been searched yet for missing people. The national guard had not reached there yet. This town of Shiogama, when looked down upon from the hill above, looked perfectly normal as if there had been no damage nor disaster there. Here there had not been a huge powerful tidal wave, but the whole shopping street had filled up with water and been ruined. All of the things for sale there were unusable garbage now. The houses had all been soaked through with salt water and would have to be completely rebuilt; they were useless. The nearby Seashore rail line had run there servicing the hotels along the seacoast with Zuigan-ji temple as a famous landmark. It had been a huge tourist area. The hot springs hotels opened their baths to all of the evacuees and other victims of the disaster. All of the people in the area were very thankful and so glad to have a place to bathe.

Passing by the typical shopping street area, we approached

Zuigan-ji temple. The area of Matsushima around Zuigan-ji was a most beautiful place, furthest in the harbor with many small islands. They had each absorbed the power of the tidal wave and had therefore saved Zuigan-ji from the strongest thrust of the tidal wave. There had been no touch of a wave there, only a slight damage to some buildings. In spite of facing the ocean, it had not been touched by a drop of water. Of course, the area in front of the main gate had been sunk into deep water, and there was much damage there. Nevertheless, the people of the area all called this the oasis of the area. Here at Zuiganji, ever since the earthquake happened, 385 people were being given a place to live, and there were 16 monks who cooked and took care of them.

We then went again in the car and went to the place where the damage was greatest of all, the Nobiru area, on the other side of Ichigahama. There was a very beautiful ancient pine tree boulevard there, but its hundreds of huge pine trees had been uprooted by the tsunami. By its sheer force, all the trees had been laid root side up, side by side in the same direction. It was as if they had each been thrown down and been placed there upside down in rows. Seeing this, we could feel the awesome and terrifying huge power of great nature.

The evacuation place where many people had run to after the earthquake, the school's gymnasium, had been completely pushed along and swept away in the tidal waves' wake. There was a Soto Zen temple there that is now nothing but rubble. There are ruins, but the main hall's roof is two hundred meters away in a river. All of the gravestones of the temple's graveyard are buried in rubble and debris. If you compare this to the lack of damage to Zuigan-ji temple, there was a great swirling whirlpool affect here that sandwiched things into its path and damaged them completely. So many people and things simply disappeared here and are gone. The degree of damage and injury to things is so great it still has not even been touched by anyone. It is from now that the various support groups and crews will begin to enter this area.

Shorin-ji is a temple nearby here, where the National Guard is staying while it works in this area. This is the last temple we visited. At Shorin-ji, there were still 100 evacuees living. We gave them all of our bread and other supplies that we had brought along. There had been 300 evacuees, but as public support came in, it became possible to move them.

So many bodies were still floating in the ocean. They were pulling them out and doing whatever they could. The crematoriums have all been damaged. Even if they wanted to cremate them, it was not possible without any fuel for the fire or any electricity available. So they have had to make open land into graves by digging into vacant lots and burying many bodies there. Priests have come even from as far as Nanzen-ji temple in Kyoto to perform the ceremonies for these burials.

That night another earthquake of magnitude 6.5 happened. Every day, again and again, the aftershocks continuously come, so that people have become numb to them. The endless lack of feeling settled in any way is in every person's state of mind at this time. In this way, we came to see how any resolution of this will be very far from now. Not only are there these myriad challenges, but that which is most feared by people all over the planet in the neighboring prefecture of Fukushima is the damage done to the nuclear power plant.

Reconsidering Life and Nuclear Power in Japan

If you look closely at the past history of this area of the Sanriku Coast, there have always been earthquakes. There are records from many eras, such as June 15, 1896 the Great Sanriku Earthquake. Also on March 3rd, 1933, there was a great earthquake in this same region with a tidal wave of more than 30 meters. The Great Chile Earthquake of 1960 created a tidal wave of 5.5 meters that struck here as well. It also created a great amount of damage.

Isn't there some indulgent point there that needs looking at carefully—this and the nuclear power plant being built in such a location, a plant that is still pouring radiation into the Pacific Ocean? There are so many points that must be seriously returned to and reviewed carefully here. There are 54 of these nuclear power plants in Japan all together, not including the many more planned to be built on already acquired land. It is because of this accident that now no one in the country wants these plants. Today, all over the whole world, the biggest problem is this. The earthquake and tsunami's challenges will be taken care of, but the results of this nuclear power plant will not go away. Scientists have called it a circumstance beyond anything that could have been imagined or estimated. They say it is an unlucky situation and these circumstances will never happen again. But it has happened now and this must not ever happen again. We must not have these. Now many voices against nuclear power plants have risen, and for Japan this is a great responsibility that has to be understood.

One very happy aspect to see through this disaster has been the people from all over the world extending their hands in kindness and their support with words from more than one hundred countries. I read these messages slowly and carefully. They are from America, South America, Africa, Europe, India, and all the various countries of Asia. I want to use this opportunity to say thank you.

Every single one of the people who train here at Sogen-ji is working intensely and wholeheartedly for this matter. For the rest of my life left, my deep vow is to cultivate them so that even one of them will be able to open the "truly seeing eye". We cannot be deceived. We cannot be deceived by what we see and the circumstances in which we find ourselves. In each and every era, we have to see from our "truly opened eye", which sees the truth, and to not deceive ourselves. This is Zen, and this is the harvest of our training and what our life is.

Thank you very much

Shodo Harada
April 11, 2011

My Struggle to Revive the Cultural and Natural Heritage of Soma in Fukushima

Rev. Toku-un Tanaka

---

*R*ev. Toku-un Tanaka is a Soto Zen priest and the abbot of Chuzen-ji *and Dokei-ji located in the town of Minami Soma, just 17 kilometers from the crippled Fukushima #1 nuclear complex. This article is from a public talk he gave at a meeting entitled, "Religious Professionals and Confronting the Problem of Nuclear Energy: Towards Sharing the Suffering of the People in the Regions with Nuclear Power Plants and Living in Interdependence", held at the Bunkyo Civic Center in Tokyo on January 17, 2012 and sponsored by the Inter Faith Forum for the Review of National Nuclear Policy and the Japan Network of Engaged Buddhists (JNEB).*

March 11, 2011

I have been entrusted as the abbot of a temple that is located 17 kilometers from the Fukushima #1 nuclear reactors. On March 11th, the earthquake hit shortly before 3:00 and was followed by the tsunami. I think it was about 4:30 as I was searching around for information through Twitter on my cell phone when I got the information that all power had been lost at the Fukushima nuclear reactors and that the diesel power that they had prepared as a substitute had been washed away by the tsunami. By chance, the year before, I was fortunate to have taken a series of seminars on the structure of nuclear power. Therefore, I knew how a nuclear reactor creates electricity and what is the most dangerous situation for a nuclear reactor. In this way, by chance, I could understand how dangerous it was that the all the power had been lost at the nuclear complex.

I immediately thought, "This is not good", but when I talked with the people in my area, such as the head of the ward and the old people in the neighborhood, they said, "No, no, there's no problem with the reactors, absolutely no problem. Don't worry." But I could not follow them. I had been taught in the study group I attended the problem of timing when all power is lost at a reactor. So for the time being I decided to keep a tab on the situation until the next morning. If the reactor could regain power by the next morning, I would be able to go home. Until then, I began to evacuate with my child.

When I started to evacuate, it was still very early, around 6:00 pm on the day of the earthquake and tsunami. At that time, no one from our area had thought of evacuating, and there had been no influence of the tsunami on our area. In this way, when we evacuated, there was a real gap in perceptions between my immediate family and the people in the area. My mother stayed behind saying, "I can't believe there will be an explosion at the reactors." In this way, my family was torn apart. There was no way to convince them.

Since up to that time I had always regarded nuclear power as suspicious, I joined that study group; and from becoming a student, I could understand. They had prepared a very big room in our area for the study meetings, but only about ten people at most joined. In this empty room, I had the chance to talk with an American man named Mike, a lawyer from America who had been doing various activities on the frontline there. He came to give a talk to our group. There were things from his talk that stuck in my mind, so this is why I was thinking it was not a good situation and decided to evacuate.

Going Back to Fukushima

My family and I evacuated to Fukui Prefecture, just north of Kyoto, where we are still now. Not surprisingly, after March 20th, I began to hear from my parishioners in Fukushima. "Please come back," they said. This was all in due course, and so I was quite resigned to it. I had already been thinking about when I would get such a request. Still, from the 20th on onward was right in the middle of the rapid flight out of Fukushima. When I got this request, my family said, "Dad, are you really gonna go back?"

I felt it was really no use to think about it too much; because the more I did, the greater the anxiety became. Naturally, I was scared of the fact I was going to be exposed to radiation. I left Fukushima on the 11th, so I knew I hadn't been exposed to what they call the "ashes of death". Even still, I thought, "Why am I going back in the middle of this situation? Is it really OK?" I was in emotional conflict, because I am human being too. Even so, I knew that I had to return. So I took the greatest safeguards for myself: paying constant attention to wind direction, I dressed in a parka, put on a mask, and made sure that my skin was not exposed.

So, I started making trips to Fukushima, then returning to my family, and then going back again to Fukushima. Gradually, I could develop some balance and little by little find a way to decide by myself what I would allow myself to do. Was I deceiving myself a bit about the prospects of becoming contaminated with radiation? This would be something I thought about after returning to Fukui. Not surprisingly, I stopped talking about such things at the moment I would enter Fukushima. This was also because my extended family kept living there. Gradually, the longer I stayed in Fukushima, the less I would wear a mask and not avoid eating certain food. I knew what was right in my mind, but when you actually go there you can't do such things. When I would visit with parishioners, they would serve me tea and say, "Reverend, do come by more often!" "Sure," I said, while in my mind I was thinking, "This water is probably contaminated." But I'm a Buddhist priest, so I should drink it. I thought I shouldn't say anything about the things that came from this whole region, so I accepted them, with thanks, with gratitude.

My work has varied due to the seasons, but as I look back now on the past 10 months, I can see that the parishioners from my area have dispersed all over Japan. With the passage of time, there has been the building of quite a number of temporary housing units in Minami Soma in the 30 to 40 kilometer radius from the reactors. It's natural that people will start getting used to living in the area and that's good, but it's surely a mistake to go back home. About 40% of my parishioners are still living outside of the prefecture after evacuating, so it's hard for me to determine where best to create a base for my work.

I've got so much stuff piled into my car, and it feels like I am moving at a snail's pace. I feel like today wherever I go is where the temple is. One day, every day, wherever I go, the number one thing is learning about people's misfortune. Amongst my parishioners, there are especially old men and women who had been in the hospital and cannot endure the lifestyle of an evacuee. I have heard of many cases where they had to be moved from one hospital to another through April, May, June, July, August, and the heat of the summer. In this situation, there was about a 50% increase in the number of deaths compared to other years.

When I hear my phone ring, the first thing I say is, "Where are you now?" Once I know where they are, I look at my schedule book and tell them my plan. Then I go see them in my car. Over six months from April through September, I've put 60,000 kilometers on my car; that's 10,000 kilometers a month. But I never noticed when I was doing it. In September, I got together with my family for the first time in two months and sent my car in for maintenance. The guy at the garage said, "You've put a lot miles on this thing." Before the disaster, my car had 150,000 kilometers on it, and I thought to myself, "I wonder how many kilometers are on it now?" When I looked it was 210,000, so I calculated 10,000 kilometers per month, which is about 300 kilometers per day—that surprised me.

All this travel was for going to do memorial services or funerals and such things. This is what I consider spiritual care for the parishioners. Conversations with them revolved around things like, "Do you have any physical problems anywhere?" or "Is there any thing the matter?" Yet every parishioner is totally different. One time, a parishioner said, "I never thought I would see the reverend again." When such words came from the face of someone I hadn't seen in a long time, I first began to cry; and then we cried together. When one cries, naturally one's feeling begins to heal and one's mind is cleared.

Reflections on Fukushima's Culture and Nature

Before the disaster, I had very strong relationships with my parishioners. The region of Soma was known as the feudal domain of Soma since the establishment of the feudal domain system with the Tokugawa regime in the early 1600s. From the Kamakura period beginning in the late 12th century up to the abolishment of feudal domains and creation of prefectures in 1871, the communities of Soma have never been moved and have been one continuous domain. There are only three such feudal domains like this in Japan: Soma, the southern domain of Iwate (just north of Fukushima), and Shimazu in Kyushu.

In this way, the Soma "family" is kind of like the emperor's family. For generations, the region has been tightly held together, especially at my temple. It is the family temple of the Soma clan. The parishioners have taken care for me and put their confidence and trust in a youngster like myself. I have been saying to everyone, "Don't just take care of me, because it is you members who have helped me grow." So there is this background of mutually being very assiduous toward each other. When I have a phone conversation with them, I think I really do have to return to Fukushima.

In this way, I began my work 10 months ago. I still go back to Fukui where my family is. In my mind, here at the end of 2011, I think that many people have come to an awareness of this issue. However, the #4 Reactor at the Fukushima facility is still in a precarious situation. My child still asks me, "Dad, are you going to Fukushima again?" As he hands me a mask, he says, "Please make sure to wear it," and I put it away in my pocket. I would put it on at the start of my trip to Fukushima, either by car or by bullet train. Then after coming back to Fukui after being in Fukushima for a week, I would realize that I had kept the mask on for only two hours the entire time, neglecting to do what I had be told.

Truth be told, when I arrive in Fukushima, driving in my car, I notice how beautiful it is. There is still just incredibly beautiful nature that is unimaginable in urban areas. It is nature that you can no longer find in Western Japan. It still exists in Fukushima, the gateway to Northern Japan. It is a great nature that you cannot escape. There is no place to journey without vegetation. Passing through such great nature in my car, I am overcome with an apologetic feeling, "I'm sorry." I think this is not the occasion to wear a mask. My heart cries out, while my mind says it's better to wear a mask.

It would be great if all the children of Fukushima could be quickly evacuated. I think if you all really think about it, the same thought will occur in your mind. When I am not in Fukushima, I think this way. But when I go back to Fukushima, it occurs to me, "I wonder what's the rate of radioactivity? Has it decreased?" This is how these two selves exist within me. I think it's some sort of gap between mind and heart. Within this same body, the mind is in one place and the heart in another. It is really just a small gap, but it seems very wide. I am still very caught up in this situation, right in the middle.

The Role of Religious Professionals in the Crisis

From September, I have gradually slowed down the pace of my work. I thought I needed to take time for myself and to place a little importance on family time. This is especially important after returning home. I had to change my feeling that such time is just as important as the time when I go to Fukushima. So during my time in Fukui, I have been thinking I should spend half the month being with my family. I have also been asked to talk about my work to people in Fukui and in the larger area of Kansai. Since November, a number of times a month when I return to Fukui, I give talks in Kyoto, Osaka, Kobe, and also Fukui on the situation in Fukushima and how to overcome the problems there.

What I am thinking about now is how in Fukushima to overcome the differences in religions and denominations among us Buddhist priests, Christian pastors, and Shinto priests. If we could be united as one, we could then go about emphasizing how important life is. I would like to see real earnestness on how to protect our children. Up to now, there has been a lot of superficial talk about this issue. We are now in a serious situation, so it is not the time to be just talking. There is no real discussion with the people of Fukushima unless you are willing to talk straight, because their lifestyle is the lifestyle of those who have been contaminated with radiation. They have lost their jobs, but still they are working, exposed to radiation. In a situation like this, we have to work to overcome everyone's differences, even though we, of course, all think differently. If you get 10 people together, they will have 10 different opinions. But this is not the time for talking in such a way. Religious professionals should all overcome their differences and overcome their different ways of thinking to unite to protect the lives of children. We need to all get together to discuss how we can love our home region and how we can restore it. In order to do this, religious professionals should really take some leadership. There is a feeling in these areas amongst the locals of really expecting something from us. In this way, my mission from now on is to dedicate myself this work and to live in Fukushima.

Transcribed by Hanae Inoue
and translated by Jonathan Watts
with Rev. Jin Sakai

What Temples Can Do as Evacuation Shelters During a Disaster

Shinobu Izawa

---

*M*any Buddhist temples were actual victims of the great earthquake and tsunami that swept the eastern coast of Tohoku on March 11, with Buddhist priests themselves also becoming refugees. Other temples right on the edge of the disaster and elsewhere in the country, however, responded immediately to the crisis. Continuing a tradition of community service, not only as designated evacuation shelters by the government, many temples opened their doors to refugees of the disaster and continued to serve them for many months afterwards. The following is a series of profiles of these temples from June 2011 provided by Jimonkoryu, a monthly journal for the Japanese Buddhist world in general and specifically for priests and temple families. Owned by Kozansha Publishers, Jimonkoryu has provided information for the practical administration of temples since 1998.

"My Duty Is to Be Someone to Welcome and Talk with": Jion-ji Temple in Rikuzentakada City

At the beginning of May, the 214m² meeting hall of Jion-ji, a Rinzai Zen Myoshinji Sect temple in the hard hit city of Rikuzentakada in Iwate Prefecture was giving shelter to 34 people from 9 families. Rev. Keiko Koyama, the 62 year-old, abbot gave the following account of his experiences:

"The temple is in a prosperous fishing village that cultivates *waka-me* seaweed and oysters. These fisher people are a bright and strong people. Even amidst such difficult conditions, they never cease to smile. All the people staying here now are temple parishioners. At times, we were providing shelter for close to 100 people. The children are precious and have taken to me calling out to me, 'Master Koyama, Master Koyama.'"

"The temple is located a few hundred of meters from the high 6-meter sea wall. At the time of the earthquake, 30 people escaped to here and took shelter at the graveyard located on higher ground. The turbid water of the tsunami washed through the temple grounds, while the main gate was washed away and nearby private homes were inundated and destroyed. All the cars in the parking lot were washed away. The floors of the temple were flooded with 10 cms of water. So it seemed that we would not be able to fulfill our designated role as an emergency shelter."

"Both the electricity and water were cut off. The road through the mountain was impassable, so for three days we were totally isolated. As the phone lines also didn't work, we depended on battery-powered radio for our news source. As we had fifty futon beds used for children's *zazen* meditation retreats and spare oil and kerosene stoves in reserve, we could stay warm. The local fire department got a hold of a generator from the flooded water, and we were able to pump ourselves potable water from a well. We also received rice from parishioners whose houses had not been damaged by the tsunami. We were able to cook rice from the propane gas tanks in the kitchen of the meeting hall. For three days, we had one meal per day consisting of a single rice ball. We had some snacks that we gave out all of that helped to stave off starvation. Luckily, there were not many victims from the neighborhood."

"This temple had become designated as an emergency shelter after the experiences that were passed down of the tsunami that hit this area during the Meiji Era (1868-1912). In this way, once a year, we performed emergency drills that became useful during this whole time. The strength of the young people in the fire department was really incredible. They were able to make a large bath from vinyl sheeting and steel barrels pulled out of the wreckage of the tsunami, so that after one week, we could begin taking baths. The refugees themselves undertook management on their own of the running of the shelter. I welcomed them to the temple and spent time talking with them personally. I didn't dare approach them like a religious leader. With each individual victim, I wanted to connect like a family member. From mid day, we would take a bath and then eat our meal together. The wives of the families would take turns preparing the meals. At the shelter located at the local gym, they slept on cardboard so some mentioned that, 'The temple is another world. They have tatami mats and futon beds.'"

"The feeling I got from this experience was that it was incredible to see how much people helped out. Today, we are still receiving material aid from all over the country; volunteers are showing up to help; and there has not been one major problem. The one thing I am really glad we had prepared for was the electric generators. It was also fortunate that we had blankets saved for an emergency and that at a temple we have lots of candles which we used when the electricity was cut. There was so much that people who live nearby did for us. It was also fortunate that we hadn't previously closed off the well. Still, there are forty parishioners whose whereabouts are unaccounted for; the main gate, the jizo statues, and other things at the temple have been destroyed; and we have little idea where to start and towards what direction we should head. However, until the final person is relocated into their temporary housing, I know that we want to provide for them."

"1,200 People Escaped from the Tsunami by Coming Here":
Senju-in Temple in Kamaishi City

Rev. Eno Shibasaki, the 54 year-old abbot of Senju-in, a Nichiren denomination temple in Kamaishi city, Iwate Prefecture had to divide his precious time not only managing an evacuation shelter but also performing memorial rites for victims who died in the disaster. His account is as follows:

"This temple is thirty meters above sea level. The tsunami came right up to the front gate. On the day of the earthquake, 1,200 people escaped from the tsunami by coming here. Beginning with the Buddha Hall, we opened up every room in the temple. We got a little more than 500 people in each room, but the ones who couldn't fit had to sleep around the temple grounds amidst the cold."

"The road to town was blocked by debris, and cars could not get through. So for three days no public aid could get in. Our first priority was 'to absolutely safe guard the lives of everyone'.

My wife, daughter, and I concentrated on working for the victims who had experienced a huge shock. I took charge of procuring foodstuffs, so I made my way through all the debris and began looking for food. At the temple, we had stored one hundred kilograms of rice for emergencies and were able to cook it while asking for help from parishioners who had not been victimized by the tsunami. Even so, on the first day, three people had to share one rice ball; on the second day, each person got a piece of chocolate; and on the third day, one person got half a rice ball and one piece of candy. In addition, each person could only get one cup of water per day. It wasn't until two weeks afterwards that we had enough food for everyone. As we had no fuel, we collected burnable debris from the nearby mountains and used it to cook rice and warm ourselves. We used the water saved for putting out fires for our living needs but didn't have enough to use for toilets. Since there were many people who had gotten quite dirty, we had to decide on rules for using water."

"Our attitude was 'to smile'. In order not to succumb to Post-Traumatic Stress Disorder (PTSD), we thought about how to have fun when at all possible. On the first day, we decided on a family council. When a victim wanted to talk, we tried as much to make them smile and to make a joke about things. Every morning, we held a chanting service, and I gave a simple dharma talk and tried to make it enjoyable. At first, people would only smile a little bit, but gradually they would burst out laughing. As a result, we could do our work in a lively and spirited way."

"On the tenth day, we were able to form a residents association. After two weeks, we still had about 300 people taking shelter who were divided in five groups. Some people were able to pump water from a mountain stream, while others collected wood for fuel from the debris. In this way, we all came to work independently. My family of three shared information at nightly meetings and carefully looked after people who seemed to have special worries. My wife is a public health nurse and was the only medical professional in the area. Sometimes she had to fly off suddenly in a helicopter at the request of the national self-defense forces."

"It has indeed been a very difficult experience, and there have been many people whose mental balance has collapsed. In this kind of situation, the important thing is that people must speak up at all costs.

We have been continuing to remind them, 'If there is anything, come talk to us.' Because of stress, it is easy for arguments to break out, so before trouble arises, I try to get in between people and mediate by listening completely to both sides."

"On March 17th, we established for the first time a Kamaishi City Buddhist Association. In order to overcome this great disaster, I was thinking that we need cooperative efforts that transcend sectarian identities. All sixteen temples in Kamaishi City and the town of Otsuchi are participating. At first the phone lines were not working, so we gathered at a Soto Zen temple to exchange information. From this point, we provided material goods for the evacuation shelters located in different places. We also provided other help like holding funerals at a Jodo Pure Land temple for parishioners from a Soto Zen temple that had been washed away in the tsunami. As we had all experienced the tsunami together, there was no sense of being particular followers of a particular sect."

"As the days of difficulty continued on, we have overcome some things. However, one particular problem has been the volunteers from the outside who do not take into account the circumstances of this area. They come one after another for two to three days, but dealing with them is difficult. Then there are some who want to leave. They need to figure out what is being asked for in this region before they start their work."

"If temples have materials on reserve for emergencies, they can overcome things, but in this situation, it wouldn't have mattered no matter how hard one had prepared. In this way, the important thing is to be mentally prepared all the time. Some years ago, this temple called on the city to become a community emergency shelter. I came to a mutual understanding and shared intention with my wife and daughter that, 'In such a situation, we will take in people who are in trouble."

"At present, there are about sixty people still taking shelter here. They are living in different areas in the temple reception hall and in an attached temple. I feel that we will help them until the last person has found a new place to live. The whereabouts of about one-third of our parishioners are still not known. The Kamaishi Buddhist Association has received the ashes of one hundred unknown persons. I feel that from now our temple would like to do as much as it can, one thing at a time."

Maintaining the Dignity of People in Such a Severe Situation: Kofuku-ji Temple in Kesennuma City

Yuko Suda is the 56 year-old wife of the abbot of Kofuku-ji, a Soto Zen temple in the hard hit area of Kesennuma City, Miyagi Prefecture. She offers the following account:

"At the beginning of May, we had 5 families of 32 people taking shelter in the large 107m² room located in the back of the temple. At first, we took in around 100 people. None of them were parishioners. We didn't have a way to divide off the room, so somehow every family bunched together. The children all cordially arranged pillows and they all slept together. It was really precious."

"The temple is a ten minute drive from the ocean. While it is not an evacuation shelter designated by the city, the teachers and children of a nearby primary school took shelter here when the 1st floor of the school was inundated by the tsunami. The parents soon followed them, and the temple turned into a shelter. They were distributed *zafuton* seat cushions and blankets for sleeping in this large room. There was no electricity, but there was propane gas, so somehow from the beginning we could serve warm rice and miso soup."

"Rev. Genpo Suda, the abbot, was very busy performing memorial services for the people who had died in the disaster, so I had to take the lead in getting help to run the shelter. One difficulty was that there wasn't enough fuel. Although it was cold, we could only use the stoves for a certain number of hours per day, so we worried that peoples' health would deteriorate. I also thought about a good balance for their food and did what I could to provide side dishes and main dishes to the rice and miso soup we gave them. It was really a great help to receive meat and fish from people we connected with from all over the country."

"In the kitchen, the mothers helped out; the men did cleaning up; and the elderly did what they could to help—all this without having to determine roles in a specific way. Everyone, including the children, did what they could do independently, and we could create a basic life style. At mealtime, the bedding in all the rooms was cleared away and tables set up. Everyone was able to sit up properly, and the children took turns every day to call out, 'Please sit up straight and put your hands on your knees.' They then bowed with palms together and said grace. Amidst such difficulty, I think we never forgot to respect each other's humanity."

"On people's birthdays, we had to be modest, but in the evening we would have a celebration. We couldn't provide a cake, but we would offer extra food for a fine meal. Yesterday, we received some beef that we grilled and with yogurt offered up a toast. We held a celebration for the children's school entrance and graduation. It is indeed necessary to have a good time amidst such difficulty."

"Through the support we have received from so many people, we have made a complete daily life. Yet we have been continuously worried about whether the food we were providing for the children has enough protein in it. In such a disaster, the thing that really helped was a gas rice cooker and propane gas tanks. I think that it would have been good if we had been better prepared beyond the gas, biscuits, blankets, and such that we had already prepared in storage. Flashlights would be another requisite."

"I try to remind myself that we need to all live together in a friendly way. Amidst flashbacks to the tsunami and being in a situation where we could not foresee when people would move into temporary housing, I think everyone dealt with their anxiety pretty well. However, whenever possible, people should talk together peacefully, and then everyone can support one another. In the end, I would like to express my heartfelt gratitude to the many people all over the country for their warm words of encouragement, their aid and support, and the way we could form strong person-to-person bonds."

Offering a Study and Training Residence to Evacuees: Joen-ji Temple in Tokyo

Joen-ji, a Nichiren denomination temple in the downtown Shinjuku district of Tokyo, offered to evacuees its eight floor Founder's Hall with two additional underground floors. Rev. Isshin Oikawa, the 44 year-old caretaker says, "It's important to give support in the disaster areas, but I was thinking, 'Can't we do something long term here in Tokyo?'" The Founder's Hall has been used as a residence for practicing monks and students from abroad. The offer has included nine rooms from the 5th to 8th floors. Two rooms are well suited for 4-5 member families with two rooms plus living, dining, and kitchen. The other rooms are $9m^2$-$12m^2$ in size. As rent, fuel, and lighting charges are free, preparations were made for bedding and cooking utensils on a rotating basis. The term for using these facilities is for one year until March of 2012, but Rev. Oikawa says, "In an attempt to respond to changes in the situation, there's a possibility to renew the term. We really want to help make these people in trouble feel secure."

Joen-ji originally planned to only accept people who had proof as disaster victims and had been introduced by a local government from the disaster areas, but they eventually decided not to require such special conditions. They did prepare a written pledge to be filled out and signed when taking up residence in one of the apartments. Rev. Oikawa said, "In this situation, it's quite difficult to get proof as disaster victims, and we thought we wanted to stand by them by making any hurdles low. As we are a temple, we are prepared to have cases of people who might be deceitful about this situation." At the beginning of May, a woman from Fukushima took up residence in one apartment, and they also received an inquiry from a pregnant woman. Rev. Oikawa says, "What we don't want to communicate to the people in the disaster areas is the need to prove their intention to us. They have their own worries and difficult battles. Just raising their hand for help is difficult enough."

At first, they opened inquires and consultation within Tokyo, but it came clear that they couldn't connect well with victims this way. So on April 17th, they began spreading information through the Internet and Twitter and distributing flyers through temples in the disaster areas. They also made contacts with the Association of Tokyo Midwives' "Going Back Home from Tokyo Project". This project gives support to pregnant and nursing women from the disaster areas who had taken shelter in Tokyo to safely return to their home areas before or after delivery. Rev. Oikawa says, "I understand that there are many people from the countryside who think, 'Tokyo is a frightening place'. They fear that if they stay at the facilities of a religious organization that they will be converted. But in the future there is the possibility that Tokyo will also become a disaster area. In a reciprocal way then, we have much to learn from these disaster victims. So we want to continue working with them as much as we can."

A Shelter for Those from the Nuclear Disaster Area:
Tozen-ji Temple in Matsudo City

"Everyone helped out, one family at a time. In this way, people have been able to purify their minds through developing such good will towards others. It's actually been really great that we became an evacuation shelter." These are the words of Rev. Etsuro Suzuki, the 52-year-old abbot of Tozen-ji, a Jodo Pure Land temple located in Matsudo city on the edge of Tokyo in Chiba Prefecture. Five days after the earthquake hit, on March 16th, this temple took in for a month 26 people from 9 households from the cities of Minami-Soma and Iwaki in the nuclear exclusion zones of Fukushima Prefecture. Speaking about the inner workings of running an evacuation shelter, Rev. Suzuki explains, "From everyday life, we could create bonds with these people from rural communities." So how did they do this?

At the time the earthquake hit, about 50 people in the neighborhood fled to the temple. 7 people who remained fearful of the aftershocks spent the night, and they offered them food. However, Rev. Suzuki says that, "Although this temple is a designated evacuation shelter and there were evacuees staying here, no confirmation came from the local government, so I scolded them for their irresponsibility." When the mayor called to apologize, he said, "I would like to cooperate as much as possible with the temple's mission of rescuing people."

The government eventually decided that Matsudo would accept refugees from the Fukushima nuclear exclusion zone. Evacuation shelters in Matsudo then began their cooperation, and city officials immediately began preparations. Tozen-ji offered the use of a large 55m² room in the back of the temple for one month until April 18th. As it was financially difficult for the temple to offer a daily supply of one bottle of tea and some rice for each person plus bedding, other temples were brought in to share the burden. Rev. Suzuki remarks, "When the temple became an evacuation shelter, it also became part of the government administrative system for refugees." If people got sick and had other problems, they had to be able to get them consultation, so they asked some doctors and nurses to come and make rounds at the temple.

On March 16th, the refugees arrived. Rev. Suzuki notes, "They seemed pretty anxious. I told them, 'We will be preparing for your dinner tonight and breakfast tomorrow here at the temple. After that, we will ask you to fend for yourselves. Every morning the temple has a basic service and chanting at 6:30, which you are free to attend if you like. It's fine to sleep as much as you like.'" The next day, everyone attended the morning service. They chanted Amida Buddha's name *(nenbutsu)* in the custom of ten times and recited the grace at the morning meal. Rev. Suzuki comments, "A young priest was concerned about what impression the very Buddhist style would have on the refugees. But I felt that they wanted something more than just a place to stay. They seemed to want emotional support as well. So we thought we should give them the flavor of what it's like to live in a temple."

Rev. Suzuki ran about collecting food, calling on parishioners and people in the neighborhood to help by bringing vegetables and other foods to the temple. Toilet paper, disposable diapers, and other necessary materials were brought by, and even a local beautician offered haircuts for free. Rev. Suzuki worked as the head of a community organizing association and played a big role in actively connecting people in the local community. In order to help out the refugees with their daily life, he posted a neighborhood map showing where they could find the public bath, laundromats, parks, and so forth. One could get a glimpse of his planning looking at the whiteboard he put up, on which were written the days, times, and contents of various volunteer services offered in the community, such as massage, calligraphy classes, tutors, and so forth.

Trying to keep in mind not to take too much control, the temple did not so much ask the refugees to do things but rather left it up to their own management. Rev. Suzuki says, "We felt it was important that everyone develop their independence. The refugees and volunteers cooperated together doing many things from answering the telephone to locking up at night. Thanks to them I encountered absolutely no problems in my own temple administration work."

Through reports of their work in the media, they were able to receive support from all over the country. They collected more than three million yen in donations, which means they received 100,000 yen per person. Rev. Suzuki notes, "It made us happy to be told, 'Your administrative work was warm and courteous.' Although there were also parishioners who had a difficult life in the midst of this situation, some offered 100,000 yen to support a single refugee." For people who could not find a place to live within the one-month time limit, the temple acted as a conduit to parishioners who were offering apartments to use.

Rev. Suzuki says the temple should continue to be an active evacuation shelter noting, "We have big rooms and a kitchen. As long as we have a public bath nearby, then we can fulfill our role as an evacuation shelter. The number of people we took in was just right. Since we only had 30 people, everyone could become friends, and each family did their best not to become a bother. From this point, we as a temple want to continue to help them for a while."

"Please Come Together with Your Pet": Ankoku-ji Temple in Koshigaya City

There were many temples that actively volunteered to take in refugees from Tohoku, but one temple made a special appeal as "a free evacuation shelter that accepts pets." This appeal was made by Rev. Yuishin Machida, the 55-year-old abbot of Ankoku-ji, a Jodo Pure Land temple in Koshigaya City, just north of Tokyo in Saitama Prefecture. He explains that, "While human life may be the number one priority, the life of a pet is also important. The abandoning of pets in the evacuation areas must have caused a lot of emotional pain for the refugees."

Some days after the earthquake, a fax was sent from the Jodo denomination headquarters saying, "We want to call on temples to take in refugees." Rev. Machida thought about another temple he runs called Jigen-ji, about a five minute walk away where there are now empty quarters in which nuns used to previously live. Rev. Machida quickly consulted the head of the parishioners association, got his permission, and then got the acknowledgment of the neighboring people. On March 20, he notified the city that they could take in refugees, while requesting for refugees that wanted to bring their pets with them. At many evacuation shelters, pets are not allowed, and there are many stories of pets being left behind at the owner's house that are painful to hear.

A local carpenter who is a parishioner was asked, "Can you make a donation (fuse/dana)?", and he built a 4.5m^2 extension for pets on to the evacuation shelter. The center itself was a living area of 37m^2, a dining and kitchen space half that size, and a toilet. Refugees were able to use the bath at the temple's parishioner's meeting hall. Food, bedding, and other basic needs were provided free through donations. There was also a doghouse installed in the garden. For those people without transportation means, the cooperation of a shipping company used by the temple during funerals was enlisted to pick up and drop off the pets. Rev. Machida notes that, "Since a priest did not live on the grounds of this place, there were no constraints."

However, after informing the city, there came no word for a month. The city administration provided information if there was a specific inquiry from any refugees, but the situation turned out that the government could not coordinate the refugees with specific evacuation shelters. So Rev. Machida independently started his own "Maneki Neko (beckoning cat) Blog" to inform people of his center. He says, "Through the power of the internet, we could really make this happen. People who hadn't seen or heard of us began to help out."

An animal hospital that had volunteered to help with decontamination efforts in the nuclear radiation zones and "elderly people who couldn't see the Internet but posted notices at evacuation centers" were some of the kinds of help that turned up. They eventually took in four families. Through good fortune, they found free apartments that allowed pets, and by the beginning of May, the shelter was empty again. Rev. Machida notes, "There are people with pets that are living and sleeping in their cars. Now that the weather is getting hot, it's going to be very difficult. There must be some people facing this difficulty among the parishioners of temples in Tohoku. If you consider this, why haven't we received any contact? We would like to do what we can for this disaster that was a once in a thousand years event."

Opening up Log Cabins on Temple Grounds:
Chofukuju-ji Temple in Chiba Prefecture

"As I am old, I would have been a burden on others if I had gone to the disaster areas, so I thought about what I could do instead." These are the words of Rev. Choshin Imai, the 73-year-old abbot of Chofukuju-ji, a Tendai denomination temple in Chonan town in the rural Chosei region of Chiba Prefecture. Soon after hearing about the nuclear incident in Fukushima, he announced to the village that he would like to accept refugees at the temple. The temple had built log cabins used for the tennis training camps at the tennis courts on the temple property. The houses are of varying size for the use of two to eleven people and are fully equipped with kitchen, bath, toilet, and bedding. Each house is suited for independent living, so there are no restrictions for families with noisy young children. The facilities can hold a total of up to 50 people. Further, as the town has many dairy-farming households, Rev. Imai contacted them and requested them to accept forty head of cattle from the refugees' own dairy farms in Fukushima. However, after two months had passed, there had been no applications by refugees to take up residence at these facilities.

Rev. Imai comments that, "It seems no applications came because our location is remote and takes time to get used to living." Still, he has this wish: "Even though were are in the countryside and it is not a convenient location, I have received voices of support from our parishioners. As we have fields for farming, we do not have problems securing food. Our village has extended an invitation to accept people from Fukushima, but we would also be happy to accept people from Miyagi as well as Iwate, so please feel free to contact us directly. We would like to extend our wholehearted support. The people of Japan are aiding all people from the disaster areas. Let us rebuild our lives by uniting our strength."

A Victim Support Matching Site:
Shinmonryu Myoken-ji Temple in Hakodate City

An offer of a second floor residence for refugees was made by Rev. Gyoki Oka, the 44 year-old abbot of Shinmonryu Myoken-ji, a Hokke denomination temple in Hakodate City in Hokkaido. After registering on an Internet matching site, he then appealed for donations to support this offer. Rev. Oka is originally from Hachinohe City in Aomori Prefecture in Tohoku and had many friends in the disaster areas. He notes, "Looking at the land that was washed away, which has a form I am so familiar with, I thought I wanted to engage in whatever long term, not temporary, aid I could. However, even though I made an offer to our city to accept victims, I didn't feel they took it with much enthusiasm. I found it irritating that the homepage of the city only discloses information about 'some public housing units' available." There have been reports from many temples of the problem of those with the will to accept victims but with a lack of positive action from the local government.

At the end of March, Rev. Oka learned about a think tank called the Dai-ichi Research Institute that operated an "earthquake homestay" homepage. It collected information and matched people offering free houses or rooms with victims who wanted to leave the emergency shelters and live independently. As of mid May, there have been 1,450 residences offered and 270 requests made for residence. There have been 85 groups consisting of 272 people who have already taken up residence. This has not only been done through offering information on the Internet but by doing matching through going into the disaster areas.

Rev. Oka's own home is two houses down from the temple and is conveniently located in the city of Hakodate. The offer is for the second floor of his residence with a 15m^2 Japanese style room and a 21.5m^2 dining and kitchen area. The entrance is shared with Rev. Oka and his family, but as it was built as a two-generation residence, the kitchen and toilets are separate. He with his wife and two children already live there, but are very much ready to accept a refugee family. Rev. Oka says, "We would like to welcome people with families that have some kind of disability. It pains me to hear that at the evacuation shelters, people feel crowded by the space both mentally and physically. We have readied some home appliances, bedding, and other things, so it's no problem to just come as you are."

Translated by Jonathan Watts
The order of temples presented in this article has been changed
from the original Japanese version by the editor.

Disaster Situation of Each Buddhist Denomination

Tendai Denomination: 1/4 of all temples nationwide, approximately 800, were damaged and 3 completely washed away by the tsunami. There were no fatalities among priests, but two members of temple families are unaccounted for. 20 temples were either partially or completely destroyed.

Shingon Denomination Koya Sect: As there are not many temples located in northern Japan, there were no fatalities or destroyed temples. About 180 temples were damaged.

Shingon Denomination Buzan Sect: More than 1/3 of all temples nationwide, approximately 1,050, were damaged, including main halls knocked out of line and minor damage like fallen roof tiles. 20 temples exist within a 30 km radius of the Fukushima #1 nuclear facility, so many of their priests and families have evacuated.

Shingon Denomination Chisan Sect: More than 1/3 of all temples nationwide were damaged with 639 temples' gravestones knocked over, 342 temples partially destroyed, 5 temples half destroyed, and 18 temples completely destroyed. 2 people died.

Jodo Denomination: 1 priest and 1 family member died. 5 temples were completely destroyed with many more than half destroyed. 8 temples are inside the 30 km radius of the Fukushima #1 nuclear facility, so many of their priests with families have evacuated.

Jodo Shin Denomination Honganji Sect: 277 temples, both large and small, were damaged. Within that number, 2 temples were completely destroyed by the tsunami.

Jodo Shin Denomination Otani Sect: 352 temples, both large and small, were damaged. Within that number, 3 temples were completely destroyed, and 1 priest was swept away in the tsunami.

Rinzai Denomination Myoshinji Sect: There was a wide range of damage with one person dead, 4 temple main halls destroyed, 3 temple main halls partially destroyed, 3 priest residences destroyed, 4 priest residences partially destroyed, and parts of both main halls and priest residences as well as temple buildings and graveyards damaged.

Soto Denomination: The majority of more than 1,200 temples in Fukushima, Miyagi and Iwate Prefectures suffered damage. Within this number, 45 temples were completely destroyed. 10 priests and family members died and 3 more are unaccounted for. In the traditional Buddhist world, the Soto denomination suffered the greatest amount of damage. 9 temples are presently evacuated due to the nuclear incident.

Nichiren Denomination: 700 temples both large and small suffered damage. Within that number, 13 were totally destroyed (1 washed away by the tsunami, 1 completely burned by fires wrought by the tsunami), and 6 partially destroyed. Other outstanding damage to affiliated groups: Hokke Honmon Lineage had 15 temples damaged, within which 4 were seriously damaged. Honmon Butsu Ritsu Denomination had over 40 temples damaged, within which 1 temple's main hall was destroyed. Unprecedented damage to roughly 100 temples that were destroyed completely by the tsunami and over 20 priests or temple family members dead or unaccounted for.

Source: The Bukkyo Times January 1, 2012

Diary of a Buddhist Based NGO's Aid Work: The Shanti Volunteer Association (SVA)

*T*he Shanti Volunteer Association (SVA) was established in 1980 when the Soto Zen denomination organized the Japan Soto-shu Relief Committee (JSRC) for the purpose of assisting Cambodian refugees evacuated to Thailand. With the completion of the emergency aid programs to the refugees by the Soto denomination, volunteers from JSRC established the Soto-shu Volunteer Association (SVA) to continue their assistance. In 1999, the association was registered with the Ministry of Foreign Affairs as a public association and renamed as the Shanti Volunteer Association (SVA); the word "Shanti" meaning peace and tranquility in Sanskrit. SVA is the oldest, largest, and most professionalized of a group of Japanese international cooperation and overseas aid NGOs established by Buddhist priests. Its core focus has been supporting educational and cultural activities in Thailand, Laos, and Cambodia, especially in educational facilities and materials to the poor in urban and rural communities. Since the Great Hanshin Earthquake of 1995 in the region of Osaka, SVA has been engaging in emergency relief work both within Japan and outside of Japan in Taiwan, Turkey, Afghanistan, Pakistan, Bangladesh, and Indonesia. From these experiences, they were prepared to quickly move into action after the devastating earthquake and tsunami on March 11th. The following are accounts of its experiences by staff working and living in the area over the past year.

March 15: Rikuzentakata - A Bleak Plain

Rev. Gido Sanbe, the Vice President of SVA, went to the hard hit city of Rikuzentakata in the far north region of Iwate Prefecture to collect information. He reported that most of the buildings which the tsunami missed still stand, but that beyond the tsunami line almost nothing exists as before. The city center was utterly destroyed and has only a few buildings standing. It is a vast expanse of bleak plain continuing to the horizon. On the 16th, SVA dispatched its Deputy Secretary General and its head of emergency relief to the region.

March 19: SVA Base Created in Kesennuma City

In Ishinomaki, another hard hit city south of Iwate in Miyagi Prefecture, bodies are still being left outside even more than a week since the disaster. So far SVA has been providing the victims with supplies and warm meals as emergency relief assistance. They believe child victims will begin to need special care as more and more frightful spectacles are witnessed. SVA created a base for its activities in the city of Kesennuma, another victimized town just south of Rikuzentakata, in order to help victims with relief supplies and warm meals from the northern part of Miyagi Prefecture to the southern part of Iwate Prefecture. On the 19th, they began sorting through relief supplies, such as blankets, towels and clothing, which they had already received.

March 20: Temples Become Refuges

People with lost families have gathered and taken refuge at not only schools and community centers but also at Buddhist temples. On the 20th, SVA delivered blankets and towels to such temples in Iwate Prefecture. SVA started to secure their own delivery trucks in order to reach other places where provisions had not arrived. SVA has also been touring evacuation sites along with members of the Kesennuma City Council for Social Welfare. The members themselves are victims of the earthquake. Even though their own houses have been left devastated by the tsunami, they work day and night for the recovery of Kesennnuma. SVA has been working with them to ensure a local, site-based approach to the aid work.

March 21: Warm Footbaths and Warm Food

SVA co-organized a program to serve warm meals with the Kesennuma City Council for Social Welfare and Yamanami, an incorporated NPO based in Mogami Town in nearby Yamagata Prefecture. Yamanami brought 25 citizens from Mogami, from high schoolers to 70 year olds, to Jonen-ji temple in the Shishiori District of Kesennuma to help cook *imoni*—a stew usually made of Japanese taro, pork, and leeks which is a specialty of Yamagata.

Meals were provided for 100 people evacuated at the main hall of the temple and for 250 people at houses provided by the Shishiori District. The volunteers also transported water from a nearby hot spring, re-heated it, and prepared foot baths. Many refugees, from babies accompanied by their mothers to elderly persons, enjoyed the warm bath. Once warmed by the meals and the baths, people started chatting and smiles spread around. Residents began encouraging one another with words like, "Thank goodness we're alive."

March 23: From Cremations to Burials

Rev. Bunmei Hayasaka, Managing Director of SVA, is himself from Yamamoto Town in the Watari District of Miyagi Prefecture, which was severely devastated by tsunami. As of March 16th, the number of dead and missing was more then 800 people in this area. Everyday the names of victims are being identified, and survivors are asking to hold memorial services even while they stay in evacuation centers. The crematorium is receiving bodies far beyond its limit, so the authorities will have to stop cremations by the end of March and shift to burials. The authorities in other towns, like Higashi Matsushima in Miyagi prefecture, may also have to make this shift as well.

March 24: Safe Havens Become Isolated Outposts

SVA supplied food, underwear, and tanks of gas to the Iwaisaki Takadai evacuation center in Kesennuma, which was provided by the 1st and 3rd branches of the Soto denomination in Niigata. About 60 evacuees now stay in the center. Perched up on high ground, it narrowly escaped the reach of the tsunami, becoming totally isolated as the surrounding area was devastated. Before reaching the center, you have to pass by the destroyed water gate and walk about one kilometer on a path where there is hardly space to step due to a mountain of oyster shells. As all roads are blocked, it is quite difficult to reach the center, and the evacuees seemed surprised and then pleased when aid arrived. The people of this area culture *wakame* seaweed and oysters for their living but lost everything in the tsunami. There is no telling when they can reconstruct their living. SVA is continuing to supply relief to these most isolated evacuation centers.

March 28: Training Volunteers

The Kesennuma City Disaster Volunteer Coordination Center was opened. SVA facilitated the setting up of the center with providing documents, receiving volunteers, getting insurance, and matching supplies with needs. A workshop for how to receive volunteers was also run by SVA for the Kesennuma City Welfare Association. As the center is not yet fully functioning, only volunteers residing in Kesennuma are accepted. However, the center is planning to expand opportunities and activities for outside volunteers soon.

March 31: Soup Kitchen

SVA provided a soup kitchen during lunch at Yonezaki Elementary School in Rikuzentakata, where the entire city was washed away with devastating damages to facilities such as banks and supermarkets as well as the town hall building. Community staff members who worked diligently for the soup kitchen were filled with smiles during the event. SVA collaborated with western cuisine chefs from the Matsumoto City Branch of the All Japan Chefs Association in Nagano Prefecture and the chief chef from a Spanish restaurant in Tokyo. Together, 200 servings were provided to the victims sheltered at the school. For three weeks since the disaster, people at the shelter took turns preparing food. With relief and smiles on their faces, they said, "So we don't need to prepare food today? OK, we'll take the day off!" Meals at the shelter had continuously been rice balls and miso soup, so the soup kitchen decided to prepare a meat sauce pasta and soup with pork and vegetables. "It's the first warm and tasty meal we've had in a long time!" One lady approached the staff after the meal and said, "Thank you so much for today. Having a warm meal reminds me of the days when we used to eat out. But I don't think we'll be able to eat out anymore. All of our properties have been washed away by the tsunami…" After spending significant time in the shelter, victims are at a loss to realize what has been taken away and are deeply concerned about the uncertainty of their lives. SVA strongly wishes that warm meals can release their anxiety.

April 6: Snacks Disappear, Books Remain

SVA is also beginning to provide soup kitchens and rations as well as mental care for children in Kesennuma. SVA has spent many years providing educational and cultural support in Asia, and is starting to implement such work in these disaster areas. Ms. Yamaguchi, a librarian at the Kesenumma City Library, says, "I think books will become a strong source of support especially during difficult times. Food disappears once eaten, but stories you've read will remain in your memory. That is why I want to deliver books to children." Ms. Yamaguchi herself is a victim of the disaster, and her father is still missing. All but one bookstore in the city were washed away by the tsunami. The only surviving bookstore also suffered damages, and its first floor is in a catastrophic condition. With prolonged sheltered life, people are beginning to develop the desire to read. The Kesennuma City Library is planning on offering routine libraries at six evacuation centers in the city. However, this will not be able to cover all 90 evacuation centers in Kesennuma. The Kesennuma City Library's mobile library car was also washed away and soaked in sea water and heavy oil, destroying approximately 3,000 books. As SVA conducts library activities in Thailand, Cambodia, Laos, Afghanistan, and Burmese refugee camps, it has begun working together with local people to run library activities for children. SVA remembers the words from one Cambodian girl from the former refugee camps, "Snacks disappear once eaten, but books can be read over and over, and that's why I like them."

April 8: Victims Become Volunteers

SVA is investigating the needs of every evacuation center in the Motoyoshi District in the southern part of Kesennuma, one of which is the need for bathing. Although baths are being provided by the city and nearby hot springs, many people are limited to once per several weeks and they want to be able to bathe more frequently. As the temperature is rising with the coming of Spring, there is an increase in the amount of dust and pollen. There are mothers who are concerned about their hair although they say, "I'm okay. Everyone's having difficult times." There are also needs for vegetables and seasoning, such as ketchup and mayonnaise, due to the limited supply of side dishes to eat with rice. Mothers in Kesennuma are used to their husbands fishing out in the ocean for months at a time, which is why they have managed to stay lively and powerful even in these difficult situations. There are some mothers who are eager to take action and travel from their shelters to the volunteer centers to register as volunteers. SVA has been planning activities to work with such locals.

April 11: Grief Care

SVA visited Rev. Seisho Shimizu, the abbot of Ryusho-ji temple and also a board member and executive officer of the Yamada International Relations Association. Rev. Shimizu has previously supported the SVA Laos office for publishing children's picture books. It is a three hour drive from Kesennuma to Yamada Town in Iwate Prefecture where there were damages from the earthquake as well as from the tsunami and fires. The area around Ryusho-ji temple was wrecked from the tsunami and fires, but the temple and the attached nursery center remained safe on top of a hill. The nursery school will reopen around April 20 and is planning on looking after 20 children. The remains of approximately 150 disaster victims were laid out in front of the main image in the temple's main hall. Rev. Shimizu said quietly while containing his sorrow, "We are planning to hold a memorial service on April 28, but there are 60 more people who need to be cremated. I have purchased white spirit tablets for each of the deceased." The first memorial service will be held for over 200 victims, some of whom are not temple parishioners. Rev. Shimizu has remained in the temple after the disaster with his wife and 14 young people from the neighborhood. "The temple survived and I will fulfill my duties as a monk", he said in his calm manner which has helped to make the people in the neighborhood feel secure. Even though the town has stopped functioning, there are people who have continued stay active and strongly pray for the restoration of Yamada.

April 11: One Month Later

Delivering supplies to evacuation centers is not just about handing out goods. It's also a great opportunity to listen to the refugees and to identify their needs. There are currently 75 evacuation centers in Kesennuma where over 6,000 people have been forced to take shelter. While investigations continue for the missing people, SVA is working together with the city's disaster volunteer center to visit evacuation centers primarily in the Motoyoshi District. At the evacuation centers, there are often complaints that the city's supplies are not allocated until there is enough for each family, hence the supplies are backed up at the city's warehouses and not delivered smoothly. Although there have been improvements, not all evacuation centers are receiving sufficient supplies. SVA is delivering supplies, such as mattresses, aluminum mats, vegetable juice, underwear, and T-shirts to those evacuation centers with shortages.

Construction of temporary housing has begun since the end of March and beginning of April. However, providing enough temporary housing for all refugees in the city is a challenge, because Kesennuma is surrounded by mountains and the ocean with little flat land. According to a refugee from the evacuation center at Koizumi Middle School, approximately half of the existing 400 refugees will be moving to Iwate Prefecture around April 12 when the new school semester starts. Refugees are worried about their uncertain future. Although there are privacy concerns, the refugees are supporting each other by checking each other's health conditions and communicating. Once moving into temporary housing, there is a risk that the elderly and invalids who can't get out often may drop out of sight. Care programs after transfers to temporary housing will then become important.

April 13: Nutrition Needs

SVA delivered vegetables from Kesennuma City's Disaster Volunteer Center to evacuation centers in the Motoyoshi District. More than a month has passed since the earthquake, and the refugees have been suffering from shortages of vegetables amidst prolonged evacuation life. The refugees were very happy to have vegetables delivered, and the elderly especially enjoyed tender turnips, Chinese cabbage, and green onions. One of the evacuation centers just received its first meat ration from the city and prepared *nikujaga*, a Japanese dish with simmered beef and potatoes. Although supplies are being brought into the disaster volunteer center, there is a shortage of vehicles and people to deliver them to the evacuation centers. SVA has been in charge of patrolling and delivering supplies to evacuation centers in the Motoyoshi District.

April 16: New SVA Kesennuma Office at Seiryo-in Temple

SVA's new office in Kesennuma was built on the premises of Seiryo-in temple in the Motoyoshi District. Thanks to their support, SVA can better deliver necessities to those in need by being based locally. SVA held a soup kitchen at an evacuation center in the Tsuya District of Kesennuma with volunteers from Funagata Town in nearby Yamagata Prefecture. To liven up the evacuation center, rice cakes were prepared from approximately five gallons of sticky rice. Rice with *natto* (fermented soy beans), rice-cake soup, and pickles were served to refugees as well as neighbors still suffering from water outages. SVA has also been collaborating with school boards from Miyagi Prefecture and Kesennuma City to deliver stationeries to 1,764 students at 11 elementary schools in Kesennuma in time for their commencement ceremonies.

April 20: Self-Reliance?

SVA held a soup kitchen at a special nursing home called Koju-en in Rikuzentakata. Koju-en has become an evacuation center where the director and staff are highly dedicated and have been continuing to accept refugees. Refugees were notified by the Japanese government to begin thinking about how to live independently after the two month mark from the disaster. A man, who had come to pick up his meal, however, told us that many of the refugees at this evacuation center are still visiting morgues in search for their family members and have not had time to think about independent living. The man said with a sigh,

"This evacuation center is filled with people who have lost their families and relatives in the tsunami. Even if they wanted to think about self-reliance, their workplace and jobs have also been lost in the tsunami." Others said, "The tsunami took away my family. I am lucky that their bodies were found. People who are able to hold memorial services for their families are fortunate." For refugees who are visiting morgue after morgue in the cold snowy weather, warm meals seem to give them comfort and open them up to speaking to the SVA staff.

May 5: Blue Sky Café and Concert

SVA held a special Children's Day event called "Blue Sky Café and Concert" at a children's playground, known as Asobi-ba, in Kesennuma. Asobi-ba is a unique playground that the International Play Association (IPA) has created with the support from local landlords as a place where the children of Kesennuma can play safely. The playground consists of various activities that children can enjoy out in nature, such as a hand-made giant slide, crayfishing, and cooking with wildflowers. During the concert, children sang along with a guitar played by the playground leader. The lively voices of the children echoed throughout the area. Two months have passed since the earthquake and tsunami, yet scars from the tsunami still remain even right by the fun-filled playground. Restoration will take time. SVA is continuing to stay close to the locals and continue its activities.

May 21: Rice Cake Making Rally

SVA held a rice cake making rally at the Asobi-ba playground in which about 200 people from the region and from evacuation centers participated. The rally was so well attended that seventeen kilos of glutinous rice was consumed by noon time. SVA held a Blue Sky Café inside the hall as it did on Children's Day on May 5. The Blue Sky Café is popular among various people from children to adults. At the same time, a small scale Blue Sky market was held at which things such as shampoos that do not need water and wet tissues were popular. Some bought them for hospitalized people, but others did so because the city water supply is sometimes unstable. Within the city, people have begun moving to temporary housing over the last couple of days after living in shelters for more than two months. On the other hand, there are still people who need to stay in shelters as they have nowhere to go. Under these circumstances, SVA is continuing to work with people in the region, so they can recover to their normal lives in the near future.

May 27: Gyocha

Volunteers from a group of priests in Iwate Prefecture called Bopennyan Tohoku and SVA held an adapted form of Zen style tea ceremony called *gyocha* in the gymnasium of Koizumi High School in Kesennuma that now serves as a shelter. During the *gyocha*, not only coffee and tea were served to the refugees, but volunteers also interacted with them. It is the third time to hold such a *gyocha* event at this shelter. At first, volunteers had to go around distributing the tea, but now people gather by themselves and say that drinking tea together makes them happy. Many have said, "Strong relationships can be built not just between refugee and volunteer, but between all individuals". The main topic about which people spoke was the temporary housing. Right after the earthquake, more than 400 refugees stayed at this Koizumi High School, but now there are less than 100 refugees. 93 temporary houses have been built, and many were able to move in. However, there are still many who do not have anywhere to go and must continue to live inside this gymnasium. For those who won the lottery for temporary housing, they have mixed feelings leaving behind those with whom they lived together for more than two months.

July 6: Kesennuma Volunteer Conference

Active NPO, NGO, and other volunteer groups in Kesennuma gathered together for a conference to discuss about collaborating with the Kesennuma District government and Miyagi Prefecture government. The conference was held at Cha Tree, a regional NPO community café. This was the fourth meeting of the Kesennuma Volunteer Conference to which 16 organizations are currently registered. While considering the activities and coverage of each of the organizations, discussions took place about at-home refugees and long-term support for evacuation centers and temporary housing. SVA is continuing to collaborate with the district government and volunteer organizations in order to provide support to refugees and to help regional restoration.

July 29-31: Disaster Relief Payments

For three days, SVA collaborated with the Kesennuma City Disaster Volunteer Center and various volunteer organizations in the city to perform traffic-control during the issuance of disaster relief payments. Approximately 9,000 households in the city were eligible for disaster relief payments. Congestion was expected, and SVA staff gathered at two venues in the city at 7:00 a.m. for traffic control. Approximately 7,500 households visited during the three days to receive their payments.

September 2: Struggles of a Female Student Volunteer in Kesennuma

Sachiko Sugiyama is a 23 year-old senior majoring in International Cooperation at Takushoku University in Tokyo. She first joined a volunteer activity at SVA's Kesennuma office on April 23. She attended a 5-week program through "Your for 3/11", a student organization established after the disaster to dispatch student volunteers to NGOs and volunteer organizations in the affected areas.

In the early stage of the program, electricity and water had not yet been restored, and volunteers themselves had to live in an environment similar to the victims living at evacuation centers. Although she has been studying international cooperation in college, this experience was a challenge for Sugiyama.

She went back to Tokyo on May 31 to her usual school life but felt strongly about wanting to work in restoration activities with the people of Kesennuma for a longer period of time. She then gave up her apartment in Tokyo and requested to re-join the SVA Kesennuma office as a long-term volunteer from August 10 through to the end of March 2012. She is deeply involved in the restoration work with the locals through activities such as visiting temporary housing.

Student volunteers at most organizations usually are only on short-term assignments averaging between one day and one week. SVA has often been told by the victims and the regional office staff that they are "sad that the student volunteers are gone soon after they get to remember their names." As one of the very few long-term student volunteers who have been actively providing support since shortly after the disaster, Sugiyama is very strongly trusted by the locals. She also contributes greatly in coordinating between communities that tend to have strong internal bonds but difficulty in collaborating with other communities. Sugiyama is known "to listen well and to be easy to talk to", so she has become an indispensible figure in the SVA Kesennuma office.

Kesennuma is famous for its fishing industry but it's also been known for having the second highest ratio of aging population in Miyagi Prefecture—36% of its population in 2008 was of the age of 60 and above. Moreover, young people who have lost their jobs from the recent disaster are leaving Kesennuma. The energy and support of young people are critical in the restoration of the region. Volunteer activities that the SVA Kesennuma office provides are needed to make up for the temporary loss of such youth power. SVA volunteers, including Sugiyama, have provided various activities such as organizing regional summer festivals at five locations in memory of the disaster victims and in prayers for restoration. SVA is continuing to provide long-term support to restoring Kesenumma so as to encourage young people to regain hope and return to the city.

October 13: Temples Share Experiences to Prepare for the Next One

SVA staff visited two temples in Kesennuma with four Buddhist priests who are members of the Soto-shu Hamamatsu Youth Organization in Hamamatsu City in Shizuoka Prefecture. Hamamatsu is located south of Tokyo near the coast, which is a similar environment to Kesennuma, and has received predictions of a great Tokai Coast earthquake and subsequent tsunamis. Therefore, the Buddhist priests came to hear stories of how each temple in Kesennuma worked as an evacuation center after the earthquake. Kofuku-ji temple was first visited. Kofuku-ji is located in one of the most damaged areas from the earthquake. Since an elementary school was located nearby, many school children evacuated to Kofuku-ji. Afterwards, these children tended to play outside and voluntary help other people. Their volunteer spirit helped people get together as a team in the evacuation center. They also prayed and performed Buddhist chanting for many of the victims at the temporary graveyard. The second temple that was visited was Sensen-ji, located in the Motoyoshi District of Kesennuma. More than 400 people evacuated here. According to Sensen-ji's abbot, there had been a more than 90% chance that such a huge earthquake would hit this area, so he anticipated opening the temple as evacuation center. He started repairing the temple and preparing for the predicted disaster in advance. One of the Buddhist priests from the Hamamatsu Youth Organization said, "Their story inspires me. I want to visit here again."

With thanks and appreciation to Rev. Shunko Chino,
Chief Executive Director of SVA, and Sachiko Kamakura,
Director of Public Relations, for their cooperation
in putting this article together.

Considering the Inter-relation between Restoration and Co-existence

Rev. Masazumi Shojun Okano

---

*R*ev. *Masazumi Shojun Okano is the President of the Kodo Kyodan Buddhist Fellowship. After graduating from Keio University in Tokyo, he received his (D.Phil.) from Oxford University in the United Kingdom and spent time teaching in universities in the United States and Hong Kong. Rev. Okano serves on the Executive Committee of the All Japan Buddhist Federation and the Advisory Committee of the International Network of Engaged Buddhists.*

After the March 11 disaster, the first thing our Kodo Kyodan (Kodosan) denomination undertook was to engage in fundraising both within and outside of the denomination. By June, we had raised about $90,000. The offerings and donations that we collected were not given to the Japan Red Cross or the government's aid system but rather to two different NGOs. One of them is SHARE (Services for Health in Asian & African Regions), an international NGO involved in medical aid. After the tsunami, SHARE first collected information in order to create a base for delivering emergency aid on a short and mid term basis. If it was possible, they said that creating a base at a Buddhist temple would be good. In this way, we volunteered the use of our Tohoku region sub temple located in Yamagata City. Being located a 40-50 minute drive from the hard hit city of Sendai, the temple could act as a base for delivering materials and medical supplies. At first, doctors, nurses, and public health workers would work for days in the disaster areas and then return to the temple for rest on a rotating basis.

Afterwards, SHARE moved their base to Kesennuma City, where the public administration was in a state of paralysis. The city hall had been hit by the tsunami, and many of its civil servants including doctors, social welfare workers, and public welfare workers had died. The town's basic information had basically been all destroyed in the damage, and so they had to start from zero. The doctors and nurses from SHARE did steady work going from house to house collecting information on the people's conditions and providing it to the city.

As the SHARE staff were engaged in these activities, we dispatched volunteer drivers from our denomination in order to help them. Day in and day out, doctors and nurses were doing hard work and then had to write reports late into the night and begin again early the next morning. The disaster areas were strewn with debris and wreckage, so accommodations had to be some distance away. In this situation, we received requests for drivers. The drivers from our own denomination worked for free for 2-3 months until SHARE decided to hire local drivers.

From within SHARE, doctors and nurses from all over the country came to work in five day to one-week shifts. Because the doctors and nurses were so busy, they tended to neglect their own health and eating habits, so it was important that they ate and rested properly. We dispatched believers and our own employees to respond to their request for having people who could look after the medical staff by doing errands and making meals. In these ways we provided background support for the medical relief work in the disaster areas.

The Connection Made through Local Performing Arts

In Kesennuma, The Japan Volunteer Center (JVC) was the first NGO group to represent the government and performed the role of acting as a volunteer center. As Kodosan has had a long time association with JVC, we thought it would be easier to do activities with them and SHARE in this area. We started providing hot meals to the victims in coordination with JVC, mostly on the weekends. Our members from Yamagata and our main temple in Yokohama as well as staff from our main office participated actively in this work.

Through this work, we made some rewarding relationships, such as during the Golden Week holidays in early May in Nami-ita, a hard hit area in Kesennuma. One such connection was with a local performing arts group. In Nami-ita, there is a tradition of local performing arts called the Tiger Dance that has continued from the Edo Period and has been designated by the government as an "intangible cultural asset". When we were providing hot meals at a village in which half of the houses were destroyed by tsunami, we found out that many of the villagers were members of the Tiger Dance group. When they discovered that we came from Yokohama, one of the leaders of the performing arts group approached me and said, "We have been invited to perform next month at the Y152 Festival for the 152nd anniversary of the opening of Yokohama Port. At first we asked the sponsors for the expenses of up to 30 people. However, at this time, we want everyone, which is more than 50 people, to participate so that it will be a sort of mental boost to get going with the local reconstruction work." While thinking that this was a good idea, I heard him say that, "We do not have enough money for accommodations for all of us." So I proposed to him, "How about you stay with us at our temple." To which he responded, "We will kindly accept." So about 50 people from the group including children and their guardians stayed with us at our main temple in Yokohama. They also performed the Tiger Dance at our temple. Through this connection, we were later able to perform a memorial service in Nami-ita during the mid August Obon festival where we chanted together from our denomination's sutras.

The traditional performing arts that took root in this region formed the core of the local identity. They have been transmitting from generation to generation their own inherited history and culture through these traditional art forms. We could feel the enthusiasm that these performers had for connecting the revitalization of their devastated communities with the prompt restart of the Tiger Dance performances.

Working to Regain Self-Reliance

Kodosan gave shelter to dozens of people in its branch temple in Iwaki City in Fukushima, about 40 kilometers from the troubled nuclear plant.

As the fear of radiation worsened in the region, about 40 people, especially young children, left the region and took shelter at our headquarters in Yokohama. After a long week during which most of the lifelines were crippled, they arrived here at the head temple and enjoyed a hot meal and warm bath. During their stay, the temple also organized games, counseling, and sightseeing around Yokohama to raise their spirits. Special lectures and programs were also organized to teach them Buddhist teachings and meditation. Some of them shared their experiences in the temple's daily testimonial sessions.

On my subsequent visit to Iwaki on April 17, I had the chance to meet and talk with a person at the city's policy headquarters. There were 1,000 temporary houses being built there. When talking with the staff from SHARE, judging from their experiences, they predicted that there will be many difficulties once they start moving victims to these units. The victims were initially housed in shelters that had no individual rooms therefore had no privacy. But the local governments were actively involved in providing them with necessary goods and food by connecting NGOs and volunteers to these shelters. Moving into the temporary houses will guarantee privacy but at the same time there will no longer be goods and food provided for by governments' involvement. The central and local governments want people to become "self-reliant" once they move into these houses, but naturally that is very difficult to achieve. Those people have lost their houses and many of them are out of work. The person at the Iwaki City government told me that the city administration will not act as intermediary for the NGOs and volunteers to work in the temporary houses because the government wants the people to be self-reliant. There is also the thinking of the government that they cannot do anything that is "unfair". For example, since offering hot meals to 200 people—which is the maximum quantity that our group can usually provide for in one operation—at a temporary housing site of 1,400 units is unfair for those who cannot receive the meal, it cannot be allowed. It seems only non-governmental groups have the kind of flexibility to perform such work. I think it will be important that this sort of work will be done by many individuals and groups working together cooperatively.

Thinking in this way, religious denominations as well should be more flexible in coming up with ways to help the people besides the normal religious services. Buddhist priests can do more than just offering support through funerals and memorial services. There could be many different ways to help people come to terms with their suffering, to regain strength to live and rebuild their communities, and to prevent them from becoming isolated and alienated.

In Buddhist based activities of helping others, we can certainly discover the spiritual meaning of generosity or giving *(dana/fuse)*. Giving is the practice of refining one's own mind and it is done for one's own spiritual benefit. The attempt for helping others may end up in failure, or others may not appreciate what you have done and may even criticize you. These are the times when we must remember that we are engaged in refining our mind. At the same time, however, we must not forget that the final goal is to help the disaster victims become re-energized, self-reliant, and happy.

"Gaining Energy"

All of our followers who became volunteers were quite delighted on their return home. They said they gained so much positive energy from the experiences. After the disaster, there were of course many people who felt they wanted to help out in some way, but not all of them could actually find something that they could do. In the case of our members, they were given opportunities to do work such as being a driver, helping with hot meals, or cleaning up debris. They also became filled with the sentiments and words of gratitude expressed to them by the victims. This is why they are delighted. When we have meetings of our support projects, usually the participants are filled with positive energy.

I think this kind of atmosphere shows the meaning of co-existence or inter-being in times of disaster. New connections come to life during disasters. When one sees the energy that comes from the connections among the victims and with the people from outside who support them, there comes some hope for the future. In recent years, we have seen the development of what is called "a society with no connections" *(muen-shakai)*. Amidst this present condition, many of us know that we desperately need to re-connect with each other, but in reality we are unable to do anything. However, in the disaster areas, there is a tangible feeling of people-to-people bonds and heart to heart connections being made. I think this has become a noble experience towards not only rebuilding the disaster areas but also revitalizing Japanese society as a whole .

This article first appeared in the Bukkyo Times
on September 15, 2011

Psycho-Spiritual Relief Work in the Tsunami Areas: An Interview with Rev. Jin Hitoshi

Jonathan Watts

---

*R**ev. Hitoshi Jin is the Director of the Zenseikyo Foundation & Buddhist Council for Youth and Child Welfare and the Rinbutsuken Institute for Socially Engaged Buddhism. Since the tragic triple disaster in northern Japan on March 11, he has adapted his skills in psycho-spiritual counseling for troubled youth and the suicidal to helping those in the disaster stricken areas struggling with trauma and grief. Rev. Jin has been making extended visits to the three prefectures of Fukushima, Miyagi, and Iwate that were directly hit by the tsunami.*

Since the tragic events of March 11th, the relief activities of numerous Buddhist denominations, their youth associations and other smaller denominational groups, individual temples and individual priests, and Buddhist based NGOs have been quite well documented. In the hardest hit areas, Buddhist temples have acted as short and long-term shelters for those left homeless by the tsunami. In Ishinomaki City in Miyagi prefecture, 4 out of 68 shelters were Buddhist temples, including the Soto Zen temple Dogen-in which was taking care 134 people at the end of April and had about 80 people into the summer months until they moved into newly built temporary housing units in early August. In Kesennuma City, also in Miyagi, 6 out of 77 shelters were Buddhist temples. Buddhist priests, not only in the disaster-hit areas but also in other parts of the country, have been very active to hold regular memorial services for those who perished in the disaster. As honoring the dead and revisiting grief through Buddhist memorial rites is a cornerstone of Japanese spirituality,[1] Buddhist priests have played an

---

[1] See Watts, Jonathan, and Tomatsu Yoshiharu. *Buddhist Care for the Dying and Bereaved : Global Perspectives*. Boston: Wisdom Publications, 2012.

important role in helping many people face the massive grief brought on by the disaster.

1st Phase Psycho-Spiritual Care: Mobilizing Volunteers

While Rev. Jin has been active in such memorial services in the disaster areas, he has been more directly focusing on offering psycho-spiritual care to those still struggling with rebuilding their daily lives in these areas. Under the auspices of Zenseikyo, he conducted three emergency training sessions in May for volunteers who wanted to help out in the disaster areas. In total, they have drawn 80 volunteers, 80% of whom are Buddhist priests from various denominations and the remaining being temple family members and lay people, most of whom are women. In such a short period, these volunteers were given basic training in 1st phase emergency counseling and support work and then came to the disaster areas for further on the job training.

This 1st phase sought to deal with the initial trauma after the disaster and adjustment to new lives in the shelters. In this way, the emphasis was on supporting people through camaraderie and natural conversation rather than direct intervention or inquiry into their trauma. When formal activities are held, they are in the form of peer counseling in groups of people with the group leader acting as an active listener rather than a psychological counselor. However, much of the work is done in a more informal style through "tea party" *(ocha-kai)* events where people share time and conversation over tea and snacks. There have also been many activities for children who may become bored and frustrated with the constraints of life in the shelters. Many volunteers have spent time with them doing "play therapy" through balloon art and providing punching bags on which they can take out pent up frustrations. Zenseikyo held a short summer camp in August in Fukushima for 70 children and 10 parents from the area affected by radioactive fallout. Many other groups held similar such summer camps, including the Buddhist NGO AYUS's summer camp in Yamanashi next to Mt. Fuji in mid-August.

A number of different Buddhist groups have been engaging in this level of psycho-spiritual care, such as the Buddhist Counseling

Group of the Jodo Pure Land denomination's Ho-on Meishokai Foundation based at Zojo-ji temple in Tokyo consisting of about 20 counselors and priests, and the Soto Zen Youth Association which has set up *gyocha* cafés for adults to talk over tea. There are also examples of local temples engaged in such work, such as the Jodo temple Sainen-ji in Ishinomaki where the female abbot and her mother use the means of delivering fish to various homes as a way to engage in conversation and support for people in the community. Unfortunately, the headquarters of the major denominations have not been able to mobilize much consistent institutional support for this kind of work.

This situation is in keeping with the general trend towards social engagement by Buddhists before the March disaster. In general, denominational headquarters have exhibited little initiative, foresight, and know-how to engage in meaningful social activities that deal with the real suffering of people. For example, the Ho-on Meishokai Foundation has been unable to create a systematic program for training counselors and have been limited by institutional constraints imposed on them by the Jodo denomination's headquarters. Meanwhile, individual priests have gone ahead and started their own initiatives, and on some social issues have started building networks either within their denominations or across denominations.

One of the special activities that Rev. Jin and Zenseikyo have been involved in is mobilizing the Japan Association of Biwa *Onkyu* Treatment Providers, a group based in Kumamoto Prefecture in southern Japan that specializes in a special form of moxibustion called *onkyu* based on ancient Buddhist Aryuvedic methods. *Onkyu* involves the heating of acupressure points and meridians through medicinal herbs, in this case the leaves of the Japanese biwa tree, which release the healing properties of the herb into the bloodstream. The elderly, who make up a large portion of the population in the disaster areas, have been the special object of this work. The treatment has served as both a substitute care for people who after the disaster have not been able to get their regular medicines and also as preventative medical and psychological care. Being sequestered in shelters for long periods of time has exacerbated the health problems of the elderly who are not able to get enough regular exercise and also suffer from stress that induces high blood pressure, heart attack, and stroke. This *onkyu* therapy helps to support both their physical and psychological stress.

2nd Phase Psycho-Spiritual Care: The Challenge of Cultivating Chaplains

The psycho-spiritual counseling shifted into a 2nd phase in the latter part of 2011 with the evacuees settling into temporary housing and dealing with longer term mental health issues during the long, cold winter months in northern Japan. This type of counseling requires more intensive one-on-one work dealing with post-traumatic stress disorder (PTSD), depression, and suicidal tendencies. This is very difficult work to initiate with local people in the disaster areas because of communication barriers due to their heavy dialect, the insular nature of their rural communities that do not open up easily to outsiders, and the lack of long-term counselors who can build trust with these people.

Rev. Jin has been trying to shift the work from 1st phase shock and adjustment care to 2nd phase trauma and grief care since September. Zenseikyo has begun running Sunday schools in the shelters where children can access trauma counseling, and they have also been setting up more "tea parties" to offer support for adults as prevention for suicides and dying alone. The past year has seen a remarkable reduction in suicides both in Japan and particularly in the three disaster centered prefectures—though the total figure still remains over 30,000 for the nation. However, experts caution that 2012 may then bring a reverse increase as people in these areas are faced with the difficulties and despair of rebuilding their lives, especially in the areas of Fukushima affected by the ongoing nuclear reactor incident. This was the situation that occurred in the regions around Osaka devastated by the 1995 Hanshin Earthquake [2].

This 2nd phase level of psycho-spiritual work has more quickly proceeded amongst the large volunteer and care community that has entered the region since the disaster. Relief workers and care givers (such as those working in refugee shelters), temple people who have offered their temples as shelters, doctors and medical workers, and especially Self-Defense soldiers who have had to recover

---

[2] Aoki, Mizuho. "Suicides top 30,000 for 14th straight year." *Japan Times*. January 12, 2012, p.2.

so many corpses, have suffered from exhaustion, burnout, and trauma in their work. Rev. Jin has especially worked with local priests and temple people who have needed support during this time. However, amongst his group of counselors there are only 2-3 people qualified to do such 2nd phase counseling work that requires professional skills and experience.

There is certainly potential for Buddhists to be more involved in this 2nd phase of psycho-spiritual work. Over the past ten years, more Buddhists—priests and temple family members alike—have become interested in developing counseling skills. The aforementioned Jodo Buddhist Counseling Group is a representative example. There is also a network of priests that has been engaging in suicidal counseling for the past five years or so. In addition, there are priests, especially in the Jodo Shin denomination, who have developed counseling skills as chaplains for the dying and bereaved. For example, Rev. Yozo Taniyama, a former Buddhist chaplain at the Nishi Nagaoka Hospital "vihara" hospice and a member of the Professional Association for Spiritual Care and Health (PASCH), has recently moved to Sendai City in Miyagi to devote himself to this work. At present, there is no systematic training system to develop chaplains run by any of the large Buddhist denominations. There exist only a few small private initiatives by concerned clergy of both Buddhist and Christian backgrounds, like PASCH [3].

Rev. Taniyama, Prof. Iwayumi Suzuki of Tohoku University in Sendai, and Rev. Jin are exploring how to develop chaplaincy training programs for Buddhist priests in part to meet this most critical need in the disaster areas. Rev. Jin has also started adapting models of Buddhist chaplaincy training already highly developed outside of Japan, such as in Taiwan and the United States. His vision is first to develop Buddhist priests to be able to truly encounter the suffering and traumatized by transforming their Buddhist learning into practical counseling and psycho-spiritual care skills. Buddhist education in Japan does not impart such practical skills, focusing rather in scholarly knowledge of the teachings and training in ritual minutia. Second, he envisions a standard criterion and certification system, like Clinical Pastoral Education (CPE) and certification in the

---

[3] Watts and Tomatsu. *Buddhist Care For the Dying and Bereaved*

United States, which guarantees a highly quality of care and the ability of those certified to engage in such work in various public sectors. In November in Tokyo and in January in Sendai, Rev. Jin through Zenseikyo ran introductory level seminars on grief care with Sister Yoshiko Takaki, the head of the Sophia University Grief Care Research Institute in Tokyo. In June of 2012, he will host Rev. Joan Halifax, founder of the Upaya Buddhist Chaplaincy Training Program in the United States, for an introductory Buddhist chaplain training workshop.

However, Rev. Jin notes that even if there were a large cadre of such Buddhist chaplains, the biggest problem at this time is the coordination of needs and services. There are not enough people right now who act as coordinators to match skilled people to the areas where their skills and background are most appropriate. In this way, Rev. Jin set up a dispatch center in Sendai City in November for Buddhist psycho-spiritual counselors to better coordinate such work. Finally, there is a need for counselors and care givers to commit to the region. Because of the aforementioned barriers to these local communities and the basic intimacy needed to do such counseling work, counselors cannot come from other regions of Japan for 2-3 days at a time and expect to be of much help. In this way, the most effective means would be to train local Buddhist priests and family members in such counseling skills. As in the aforementioned case of the Jodo nun in Ishinomaki, such local priests and temples have long established ties to their communities and can most readily offer the kind of psycho-spiritual support they will need in the coming years.

The Deep Listening *Gyocha* Volunteer Activities of the Soto Zen Youth Association

Rev. Taiko Kyuma

---

*R*ev. *Taiko Kyuma is the former Chief and now Advisor to the National Soto Denomination Youth Association as well as Advisor to the Association's Department of Disaster Aid and Revival. He is the abbot Ryutoku-ji temple and the vice abbot of Jorin-ji temple located in Da-te City, Fukushima Prefecture, on the edge of the nuclear exclusion zone.*

On the day of the earthquake and tsunami disaster, the National Soto Denomination Youth Association (SYA) established a Department of Disaster Aid and Revival. At first, we tried to gather as much information as possible despite extreme difficulties as communication had been disrupted in the disaster areas. Our work at first was to give utmost priority to material aid. Receiving requests for emergency material aid, we began delivering this aid on March 17 for the maintenance of living in the six cities of Shirakawa, Izumizaki-mura, Sukagawa, Tamura, Fukushima, and Da-te in Fukushima Prefecture. We then established a local headquarters of the Department of Disaster Aid and Revival in my own Jorin-ji temple in Da-te in order to create a base for our work and regulate it according to locale and information we were collecting. The objective of our work in these localities was to strive to develop cooperation among the government offices established for disaster relief and the social welfare associations in each region.

From this time, SYA, with 64 branch groups consisting of more than 1,800 members, has engaged in a number of activities, such as: material aid, basic volunteer support, rehabilitation of temples, chanting and memorial services for the dead, deep listening *gyocha*, a *Kanze-phone* telephone consultation hotline, a "correspondence project" to prevent the isolation of individuals, a proposal for workshops on aid for self-reliance at the newly built temporary housing, a summer camp for refugees from the nuclear incident, and decontamination work in the nuclear affected areas.

From the standpoint of being Buddhist priests, we have sought to maintain a self-awareness of the importance of compassion *(maitri-karuna/ji-hi)*, yet at the same time not imposing our spiritual views when coming into contact with victims of the disaster. I myself have been influenced by the important idea of "a volunteer being a catalyst" from the former Managing Director of the Shanti Volunteer Association (formerly Soto-shu Volunteer Association - SVA), Rev. Jitsujo Arima[1].

Deep Listening Gyocha in the Disaster Areas

The term *gyocha*, literally meaning "tea practice", is a ceremony of taking tea conducted in Zen temples and Zen practice centers. Tea is taken in a simple and direct manner in order to objectively re-examine one's own practice and one's own daily existence through conversation with one's Zen master and co-practitioners. This is a very important time for the practitioner to develop mindfulness and to return to one's own essence. *Gyocha* as an activity in deep listening to victims during a disaster is about holding and embracing the physical and psychological stress of the victims and offering them a chance for respite while being caught in unavoidably constrained circumstances with no immediate prospects for their future. In this way, we have sought to develop mutual communication as companions experiencing this same life. In terms of the daily drinking of tea in the disaster areas, our activities have aimed to help the victims slowly recover their own beings and way of daily life through sharing tea and dealing with the difficult reality together.

Gyocha for supporting victim revival during disasters was started by SYA at the time of the March 2007 earthquake on the Noto Peninsula in Ishikawa Prefecture. The opportunity leading up to this application of *gyocha* came from the experience of providing hot meals at the time of the October 2004 earthquake in the Chuetsu region of

---

[1]   For a brief profile of Rev. Arima and his importance to socially engaged Buddhism in Japan, see: Watts, Jonathan. "The Search for Socially Engaged Buddhism in Japan". http://www17.ocn.ne.jp/~ogigaya/keio/jsebcs.htm

Niigata Prefecture. At that time, a woman made a comment to one of our members, "We are thankful to receive the hot meal, but as you are a Buddhist priest, we victims would like you to listen deeply to our stories." Afterwards, we asked our SYA members what they could offer and called to their attention the importance of secondary volunteer activities involving "deep listening". We then set up a study group to prepare for such work and then began the first *gyocha* during the Noto Peninsula earthquake. In the same year, another earthquake hit the Chuetsu region, and we ran more *gyocha* there as well.

Gyocha activities have the following specific aims:

• *Offering hot tea for the physical well being of disaster victims:* In disaster areas, resource lifelines have been knocked out and there is a lack of fuel, so it is a real problem to prepare hot meals. The work then is also concerned with the physical health of the victims.

• *Deep listening and mental and spiritual care for the victims:* Our volunteer staff, which at first was all Buddhist priests, engages in deep listening to the concerns of victims. When a disaster takes place, we make efforts to begin work with as many personnel as possible as quickly as we can in order to deal with the anxiety and variety of emotions that the victims experience.

• *Providing a system to connect government and volunteer center support for the needs of the victims:* In order to connect the government and volunteer centers' work, we go on rounds of each evacuation shelter to listen and ascertain needs; for example, at public recreation centers, the need for futon beds for people with back pain and simple changing rooms for women who need privacy.

• *Supporting communication on all levels:* Through *gyocha,* we strive to develop communication among communities and person-to-person communication as well as supporting the self-reliance of the victims and the communities in the disaster areas. We introduce fellow victims to each other and support their deepening relationships as well as proving active support for making connections from the individual to community level during *gyocha*.

With the passing of time after the disaster, the evacuation

centers became filled with plastic bottles and cans of water and tea. However, we did not want to do *gyocha* using these drinks. Rather, we pay special attention to the process of a person preparing tea or coffee by hand, the smell of brewing, and the "warmth" of other humans that they may have almost forgotten.

Reflections on the Practice of Gyocha

Creating a *gyocha* can be done relatively easily, but within the limits of what you can get in a disaster area, you need to prepare some in advance. Preparation involves: 1) preparing materials, 2) determining the location and how to adapt to it, and 3) confirming the volunteer staff and what they can do. Further, you have to get an estimate of the number of people at an evacuation center and consider the day and time of the *gyocha*. When doing work at an evacuation shelter, there's a difference between the real number of people and the figures of the data of victims. There are changes everyday. For example, at a center with 100 people, many come and go throughout the day, so in reality you end up dealing with up to 30 old people and children at one time. In this way, the needs expressed during *gyocha* are not all the needs of the place. Young people are young people; women have women's needs. I think it's a good idea to listen deeply when there is a discussion about the needs of the those who are absent.

At one center, there had been many people at a *gyocha* we did, and we felt we were quite successful in this way. However, the next time, there was only one person besides us. He was filled with despair, so I felt I wanted to get intimate with him and support him. The ideal of this work is that when getting intimate with the real suffering of people, you can support them a bit mentally and emotionally.

There is no need to talk to someone who is resting and won't be woken up. However, when talking with the person next to them, it's important to examine the situation and ask the evacuation center staff about their situation. There are people who have developed problems in the legs and back and can't move without pain. The aim of our work is to be concerned for their health and lifestyle and not to lose contact just because they are resting. We should communicate with people in charge and tell the medical staff or shelter staff about anyone who seems in poor condition. There are many instances of a "just wait" attitude in dealing with people's demands and requests, so we try to fill in the gaps and fulfill the role of connecting people. This is one significant aspect of *gyocha*.

At the evacuation centers, living is naturally in a shambles, and each person has to make their life in one little corner. There are many people dealing with stress who will not greet or offer any expression to us. This is especially due to the high rate of turnover amongst the centers' staff, the number of uninvited media who show up, and the many other visitors including volunteers. There are also cases of stress being caused by too many activities being run. While victims continue to deal with this stress, they can also appreciate the kindness of a Buddhist priest.

However, in reality, in such times of disaster, there are specific religious groups that take advantage of the situation by engaging in prosthelytization and profit making activities. At the evacuation centers, there are many religious people from various denominations. At public evacuation centers, I have heard of people using the name of a certain denomination and seen people with robes and a priestly appearance engage in persuasive prosthelytization and self-advertising. Those people have been denied access to such evacuation centers and had their volunteer activities forbidden by the local social welfare volunteer center.

Master Dogen said in the *Shushogi*, "The Buddha himself lived as a human being before attaining Buddhahood." In this way, it is ideal if a priest can humble himself to develop a heart-to-heart connection with a disaster victim. In the case of being asked to come do chanting and give a dharma talk, we should do it rather privately, refraining from doing it in the evacuation center or in front of many people. If the person has a family temple, it's important to help make a connection to it. In reviving local community, people who come from the outside must desire to make a connection with the local people. In this way, we think it best that even at large evacuation centers the number of *gyocha* staff should not exceed ten persons.

After doing *gyocha* many times in a place, one may end up

asking the same thing to someone like, "It sure is hot today" or "This is my favorite snack, and what is yours?" That person ends up feeling embarrassed and doesn't want to respond. It's necessary for the volunteer to figure out a way to deal with this. There may be children running around playing energetically, but we must be careful to notice their mental pain and the lack of brightness in their eyes. If the *gyocha* volunteer staff can help by bringing to each *gyocha* some of their own local snacks or travelling gifts and offer them to the victims, then this will provide a point of conversation to connect with them. This seems to be effective in creating a bond without having to worry about what to talk about.

Deeply listening, you can observe a person's discontent, dissatisfaction, insecurity and anxiety. After sincerely experiencing the life of a victim in both body and speech, afterwards we make a report to the volunteer center on the specific details (daily life, illness, etc.) of the person. For example, when one asks to a victim, "Are you having any problems?" and he says, "I am doing okay... Thank you very much for the tea", one should not be satisfied with that response and end the conversation. To the person who says, "I am not feeling burdened," I say, "In that case, is there anyone around you who's having problems?" Then listening, I take down information on their reply which begins, "That person over there..."A person holds in some suffering that remains unspoken towards other people. They will not directly say to someone they have just met, "Please help me." It's a mistake to think the meaning of *gyocha* is simply a way of getting intimate with such a person's real feeling to do a "needs assessment". While drinking tea, we listen deeply, making person-to-person connections and connections with local people. In order to revitalize local community, someone needs to notice when there is a person who can carry out this role in the community. This is something we want to help with.

Conclusion

Gyocha has been recognized by wider society as the work of Soto denomination volunteers. We are receiving many requests to do such work from the volunteer centers of social welfare associations and from local governments. We want to respond to such requests, offer support towards the revival of these communities, and assist victims to re-establish their self-reliance. However, with the passage of time, people are returning to their homes, moving to temporary housing, or moving away altogether, and the lives of the victims are undergoing a metamorphosis. Volunteer centers are being scaled back and offices being relocated as the disaster areas shift into a new phase of rehabilitation and restoration. *Gyocha* is also undergoing a change from when we started doing it. I think from examining the needs of the disaster areas, we will make a change in our methods of operation and search for a new sustainable course. There might be occasions like festivals where we are asked to join. Especially in the regions where our volunteer staff have established strong footholds, we will take on cooperative work for community events. It's nice if we can connect people in communities together while drinking tea. However, if people in communities themselves can come together to drink tea and talk as a way to revive the community without *gyocha* volunteers, then *gyocha* can discontinue its work. When that time comes, donating equipment to community centers and regions can be a course of action.

Translated by Jonathan Watts with Rev. Jin Sakai

"Let's Have Fun in Aizu!"
Smiles on the Faces of the Children
of Fukushima

Rev. Eka Shimada

*T*he Zenseikyo Foundation & Buddhist Council for Youth and Child Welfare in association with the Soto Zen denomination's Fukushima Branch Youth Division held a two-day summer school camp called "Let's Have Fun in Aizu" from August 2-3, 2011. The participants were primary school children from Umizoi village on the coastal area of Fukushima, which was devastated by both the tsunami and nuclear reactor incident. The plan was to invite children, who since the triple disaster in March have been restricted to playing indoors only, to run around outside and play freely. There were a total of 64 children from the ages to two to primary school grade six. Rev. Eka Shimada is a Jodo Pure Land denomination female priest. She has been helping Zenseikyo's relief work since March 11th, but has been involved for a few years with the Association of Priests Grappling with the Suicide Problem and the Hitosaji Association which feeds the homeless in Tokyo.*

Feeling Alive amidst Great Nature

When we first all gathered, there were some kids who were trying to hide their nervousness. But once we got on the bus, we introduced ourselves and played games, and eventually the kids began to smile and the staff could become at ease. Our itinerary of two days and one night took us to the heart of Aizu Wakamatsu City in western Fukushima where there are no worries about radiation contamination. On the first day, we visited the lush and green Sayuri Park where we had a program of outdoor recreation, such as swimming and climbing on a ropes course, as well as a barbeque. Blessed with blue skies and high floating clouds amidst great nature, the kids could run all over the place and work up a good sweat.

At night, we stayed at the Fukushima Aizu Nature Home. We expected that the kids would be a bit disoriented with the many rules of staying in a public lodging place. But after listening to the explanations of the home's staff, the kids set up their beds, followed the guidelines, and helped each other to pass the time quite naturally.

During the opening ceremony the next morning, the Buddhist flag was raised and a flower offering was made. Then while singing together in one resounding voice the Buddhist hymn "Witness to Veneration" (sasagu-miakashi), we made a vow to achieve our goals for the two days we had gathered to be together. Finally, with the bringing together of recollections from each hometown, white flowers were offered.

At the dinner that followed afterwards, everyone chanted the Buddhist meal offering known as the Verse of Five Contemplations (gokan-no-ge). For the children to understand better, each of the verses was spoken in a modern translation form. The children put their hands together saying, "The food we put in our mouths comes from the lives of others for which we give thanks." After dinner, everyone gathered around a big campfire for folk dancing and entertainment. At the end, some of the priests in a surprise move began to dance around singing the theme song of the children's favorite television show called Marumo-no-okite (Marumo's Rules). The kids eventually all joined in a huge climax to the evening. As the coals of the fire started to turn white and die down, the children began to notice the starry night sky and their faces lit up with smiles. It was a very lively and warm time together.

When it was time to go to bed, their excitement continued on in the unfamiliar setting of sleeping in bunk beds, and for a while, they could not sleep. However, with the help of the fatigue of the days events, the children calmed down and fell into the deep breathing of sleep.

A Day of Touching History and Tradition

Our second day began with gymnastics and stretching. At breakfast, the children started getting used to reading the Verse of Five Contemplations aloud. It was remarkable to see their adaptability. We then broke up into teams and walked around the vicinity of the Nature Home, examining the different trees and practicing orienteering. Eventually, we founds ourselves climbing up and down on mountains paths and rambling along in the nature.

After departing the Nature Home, there were many kids who enjoyed the visit to the Tsurugajo Castle in Aizu Wakamatsu City. The children could see and get a feel for the real weight of the muskets and the Japanese swords used by the old samurai in the exhibition area. They also learned about the famous White Tigers, a clan of local samurai who led the revolution against the Tokugawa Regime in the mid 1800s. We then climbed up the castle tower where we got a panoramic view in four directions of the beautiful green area of Aizu Wakamatsu. Feeling the breeze against our sweaty bodies and taking this all in was refreshing and wonderful. Finally, we provided them some time at the gift shop in the castle to purchase some travelling gifts with their pocket money. They seemed to be quite serious in choosing something memorable for themselves and their families within their budget.

The next place we visited was the Aizu Nisshinkan School for young samurai that was established in the final years of the Tokugawa Era as part of a system for educating young men. The White Tigers were taught and raised here under the very strict rules called *ju-no-okite*, summed up in the phrase, "These are the things that must be done" *(naranu-koto-wa naranu-mono desu)*. Although it wasn't clear whether the students understood them exactly, many exclaimed, "Wow! That's really strict!" Many could not hide their surprise to learn about the earnest attitude that young people their same age had in this region over 100 years ago.

After filling themselves on local food served in a traditional round wooden lunch box, the children split into groups by choice to do either archery or painting. For those who did painting, they were asked to consider how their local regions might recover from the present situation and to decorate one of the self-righting pop-up dolls as a good luck charm. The kids began to use different colors to draw the faces and kimonos on the dolls and seriously thought about different patterns while carefully moving their pens along the surface.

After this activity, everyone got back together to practice Zen meditation. The openhearted Zen priests who were acting as staff went off to change and when they reappeared in the meditation hall in their monastic robes, the students immediately took on a more solemn air. After receiving guidance in how to cross their legs and place their hands, they concentrated and meditated amidst a peaceful atmosphere. Once the children could get used to sitting in this posture, they began to light up with a sense of accomplishment in their endeavor.

At the closing ceremony, the staff passed on words of encouragement to the children who were living in a situation where they could not freely play outdoors in their home areas. After giving out certificates of completion, the entire schedule came to an end.

The Present Situation of the Children

Despite the enjoyable time we had at the camp, for the children, there still must have been some anxiety in being away from their parents and their home for the first time since the March disasters. The earthquake and the tsunami came up in discussions with them, and we could see that the anxiety in their minds still lingered a bit. We also heard about their complicated and lonely feelings towards having to transfer in and out of schools. But it was great to see their resolution to make new friends after leaving their old schools.

Getting a little distance from these difficult feelings, I feel that taking this opportunity for both the children and us guardians to have fun outdoors without anxiety was very important. Being together for only two days was short, but by connecting with these well-behaved children, I could feel the blessing of how these children may find joy rather than misery in their future.

Translated by Jonathan Watts
from Pipala Magazine September - October 2011

followers of Chuzen-ji in Minami-Soma clean
temple in October amidst ongoing radiation

refugees from tsunami live in the Buddha hall of Senju-in
temple in Kamaishi

Rev. Masazumi Shojun Okano visits tsunami survivors
in Nami-ita

Rev. Jin Hitoshi takes part in a tea party with survivors in Miyagi

a Soto Zen Youth Association *gyocha* event

a young boy from Fukushima practicing meditation at the summer camp in Aizu

Rev. Tetsuen Nakajima

Rev. Hidehito Okochi

Pure Land Buddhist flag opposing
nuclear energy and armaments

the hand drum of the *daimoku* of the *Lotus Sutra* at an
anti-nuclear rally in Tokyo

Monks and followers of the Nipponzan Myohoji gather in Tokyo for
an anti-nuclear rally

the solar panels of Juko-in temple in Tokyo

Kenju-in temple in Tokyo rebuilt
with eco-friendly materials

the Dalai Lama greets survivors at Saiko-ji temple in Ishinomaki

PART II

BUDDHIST SOCIAL TRANSFORMATION

Confronting the Nuclear Issue and Envisioning the Future

NUCLEAR POWER IN JAPAN

Fifty-four nuclear reactors supply about a quarter of Japan's electrical energy needs (**1**). Before the Fukushima disaster struck, new reactors and energy conservation were set to double that proportion by 2030 (**2**).

1 Nuclear landscape

■■■■■■■ Kashiwazaki Kariwa (TEPCO)

■■ Shika (Hokuriku Electric)

■■●● Tsuruga (Japan Atomic)

■■■ Mihama (Kansai Electric)

■■■■ Oi (Kansai Electric)

■■■■ Takahama (Kansai Electric)

■■◣ Shimane (Chugoku Electric)

●● Kaminoseki (Chugoku Electric)

■■■■ Genkai (Kyushu Electric)

■■● Sendai (Kyushu Electric)

Ikata ■■■ (Chubu Electric)

Tomari ■■■ (Hokkaido Electric)

Oma ◤ (J Power)

Higashidori ■● (Tohoku Electric)

Higashidori ●● (TEPCO)

Onagawa ■■■ (Tohoku Electric)

◎ Earthquake epicentre

Namie-Odaka ● (Tohoku Electric)

Fukushima Daiichi ■■■■■■ (TEPCO)

Fukushima Daini ■■■■ (TEPCO)

Tokai Daini ■ (Japan Atomic)

Hamaoka ■■■● (Chubu Electric)

JAPAN

Nuclear reactor status

■ Accident with nuclear fuel damage (4)   ■ Not affected by earthquakes (40
■ Accident without nuclear fuel damage (2)   ◣ Under construction (2)
■ Safe shutdown (8)   ● Construction planned (10)

2 Energy mix

	Oil	Coal	Gas	Nuclear	Renewables

2007	136	261	282	264	88
2030 (estimate)	113	136	537	214	21

0   200   400   600   800   1,000   1,20

Power generation, TWh

The Choice of Development Paradigms in Japan after the 3/11 Fukushima Nuclear Disaster

Jun Nishikawa

Jun Nishikawa is a Professor Emeritus at Waseda University in Tokyo. He was the Research Director of its Graduate School of Asia-Pacific Studies from 1998 to 2007 and is Advisor to the Institute of Taiwanese Studies at Waseda University. Prof. Nishikawa is one of the leading development economists in Japan while also taking a keen interest in alternative development and economics, especially "Buddhist economics". This paper was first presented at the biannual conference of the International Network of Engaged Buddhists (INEB) held in Bodhgaya, India, October 26-29, 2011. The author thanks the participants in the workshop session on "Buddhist Economics" for their useful comments to the original version of this paper.

Introduction

If disasters were only caused by tsunami, we can always restore our lives, even though we have a very severe and sad experience from it. However, when disasters are caused by radioactivity spilled over from nuclear plants, we don't know how we can restore ourselves.

– a refugee from Minami-Soma town in Fukushima Prefecture, November 2012

The northeastern part of Japan was hit on March 11, 2011 by an earthquake of magnitude 9 as well as a huge tsunami that accompanied it. At the same time, at the Fukushima No.1 Nuclear Power Plant, the meltdown of fuel occurred in reactors #1, #2, and #3 due to the loss of all electrical systems, which stopped the cooling systems in these nuclear reactors. On March 12 and 14, the containment buildings of these reactors were destroyed due to a hydrogen explosion caused by exposure of the nuclear fuel in these units. On March 15, reactor #4, which had been shut down for inspection at the time of the disaster, also had a severe incident. Its containment building was also damaged due to a hydrogen explosion caused in the stock pool of used fuel in the reactor.

In the following days, highly radioactive materials were emitted by successive explosions at the facility as well as by exposure of melted fuels into the atmosphere. The contaminated water was also leaked into the sea. At first, the radioactive emission was declared to be 4th degree but later modified to 7th degree, which corresponds to the explosion of the Chernobyl Nuclear Plant in the Ukraine in 1986.

In this paper, we will first look at the basic reasons why atomic disasters are caused at the time of natural disasters, such as during a huge earthquake and tsunami. The Fukushima incident was a human-made disaster, which was the consequence of a development policy that prevailed in Japan during the era of high economic growth and world-wide competition for material affluence. Japan's energy policy was handled by the dominant ruling elite composed of a politicians-bureaucrats-business group coalition. In particular, in the field of nuclear energy policy, the so-called "atomic village", composed of the above-mentioned coalition plus academic elite and mass media, dictated it. In contrast to the dominant governing elite, the common people who had conducted peaceful lives until the disasters became the first victims. However, the entire life system of Japan as well as the whole earth have seriously been damaged by the severe incident.

Secondly, we will look at the rise and confrontation of two oppositional views for the development pattern of Japan after the "East Japan Great Disasters". One is the continuation of a top-down and centralized type of development policy, which accepts economic globalization and free trade market policies. The other is the newly emerging, endogenous type of development policy, which emphasizes regional sovereignty, use of local resources and recyclable energy, and is supported by the participation of civil society. We will see that the former development paradigm is closer to one of violence towards all living systems, which will be unsustainable in the end; while the latter might lead to a more convivial and peace-oriented society.

Thirdly, we will look at the role of Buddhism in this confrontation of different paradigms. After the Meiji Restoration in 1868, Buddhism in Japan was marginalized from political and social life. Buddhist temples have come to be used by the public only in times of funerals and consequent memorial services. Therefore, Japanese Buddhism has been called "Funeral Buddhism". It has lost most of its spiritual mission. However, since the time of the 3/11 Disasters, Buddhist temples and priests have provided places for refugees as well as caring service. These are signs of a revival of the spiritual mission of the Buddhism. This is a time when the Japanese, after decades of economic growth, have started to seek a lifestyle corresponding to a post-economic growth period. In this way, we will see that the notion of development in the teaching of the Buddha—which advocates abandoning the greedy life for one of the fulfillment of spirituality—can provide guidance in this transitional period. Buddhism condemns a top-down and centralized type of development *(pattana)*, which increases the acquisitive mind and greed, and shows way to reach development from within and spiritual fulfillment *(bhavana)*.[1] This teaching can show the Japanese the right way in this time of conflicts over different development paradigms. Buddhist wisdom can be useful and vital in the contemporary age when people are in search of their life choice after the 3/11 East Japan Great Disasters.

The Nuclear Disaster in Fukushima: The Consequence of a Development Policy

In these disasters of 3/11, approximately 20,000 people lost their life or are still missing in the three prefectures of the Northeast (Iwate, Miyagi and Fukushima). At the same time, half a million people in these prefectures lost their relatives, houses, neighborhoods, and community life. Many people experienced some if not the total destruction to their homes and belongings. They lost their workplace and jobs as well. In Fukushima Prefecture, where the nuclear explosion took place, from

---

[1] *Pattana* is a Thai word meaning "development", most often used for modern economic development. It derives from *vattana* from the classical language of Buddhism, Pali, meaning an increase in number that may spread like a weed. *Bhavana* is another Pali term that means "meditation", "cultivation", or "development" in qualitative terms, as opposed to *vattana* which implies development in quantity. The interpretation of *pattana* and *bhavana* in terms of modern economics is based on Phra Payutto (1995) (1996).

March to June, over 200,000 people (10% of the total population of the prefecture) were obliged to evacuate to other places, half of them outside the prefecture.

The government ordered the inhabitants of the surrounding area of a radius of 20 kms from the nuclear facility to evacuate themselves and recommended those living in the area of a radius between 20-30 kms to remain inside their houses. However, later it was discovered that hot spots of contamination exist even in the area of a radius over 30 kms from the reactors. These were created due to a westerly wind and rain several days after the incident. There are many people, especially, pregnant women and families with small children who chose voluntarily to evacuate outside this 30 km zone.

In this way, this nuclear disaster has destroyed family and community life. It has also shrunk the economic and social activities of the region. In addition, we cannot forget that the coastal areas were also seriously damaged by the tsunami. The radioactivity[2] contaminated the soil, water, and living systems of the region and also threatened life in other parts of Japan, including the capitol of Tokyo. Here we have to see the reason why the nuclear power plants have caused such serious damage, and understand why this incident was not a natural disaster but a human-made one. It is the consequence of a deliberate development policy geared towards high capital accumulation adopted by Japan after WWII.

The Northeast part of Japan is one of the poorest parts of the country. It provides the role of supplier of agricultural and marine products as well as labor force for Japan's metropolitan, industrial center of Tokyo. It also provides the role of energy supplier to the latter. The power structure of this country in the post-war era deliberately decided to emphasize among energy sources nuclear energy. It was believed to lessen Japan's dependence on oil imported from the Middle East and to open the road for nuclear armament for this country.[3]

---

[2] cesium134 has a half life of 2 years, cesium137 half life 30 years, iodine131 half life 8 days, and others.

[3] The necessity of nuclear development in order to prepare for possessing nuclear arms was never officially acknowledged. However, the necessity to hold and develop nuclear technology as a "first-rank" developed nation has always been declared by politicians of the Liberal Democratic Party (LDP), which ruled Japan for most of the post-war era. A national public television (NHK) special program recently disclosed the connection of the latter intention to a rearmament strategy. NHK Special Team, *Kaku Taikoku-wo Motomete (Desiring to be a Super Nuclear Power)*, Tokyo: Kobunsha, December 2012.

What is this power structure in Japan's high economic growth period? It is the complex of a politicians-bureaucrats-business world. They represent a policy of *pattana*, centralized development conducted from above. *Pattana* in Japan has emphasized high capital accumulation and consumption through an export-oriented strategy. An international and domestic division of labor policy was adopted to realize high economic growth in this country. This policy was characterized by a division of industrial centers and peripheries, supplier of resources to the former. In order that this strategy be accepted by rural areas, two policies were adopted: 1) an economic policy of huge "subsidies" or aid were injected in the latter, in particular, in areas that accepted nuclear plants; 2) a cultural policy of huge propaganda advocating that "nuclear plants are always safe, bringing prosperity and a bright future to a region". Thus, 54 nuclear plants were constructed in the peripheral, rural areas of Japan, mostly in coastal areas in spite of the fact that the archipelago of Japan is located on the earthquake belt of the Western Pacific.

However, the problem was that the power structure in Japan—in particular the nuclear power structure or so-called "atomic village" composed of politicians, bureaucrats, big electric companies, scientists and media, the last two being thickly fed by monopolistic electric companies—believed themselves that nuclear power plants were absolutely safe and forgot to prepare for a large-scale earthquake. The 3/11 earthquake with a magnitude of 9 had already been forewarned by scientists, even in internal reports to policy makers and the Tokyo Electric Power Company (TEPCO). These warnings, however, were ignored, and the 3/11 tsunami of a height of 14-15 meters at the sight of the Fukushima #1 facility easily surmounted its barrier of 7 meters— a scenario also forewarned by some seismologists. Thus, the nuclear incident at Fukushima #1 was clearly a human-made disaster and not a natural disaster.

Who are the victims of this severe incident? First, local communities in the neighboring region were seriously affected. At the time of the earthquake and tsunami, the local communities showed the strength for mutual help, but they are now broken up by forced evacuation. Many people are suffering from isolation from their neighborhoods and home regions. Families themselves have often been obliged to be separate. 200,000 displaced people are not certain when they can come back to their homes or if they can ever come back to the home region. Many people have lost their workplace, school, and neighborhood life.

Pregnant women and families with small children fear that their children will suffer from radioactive materials emitted in the region. Thus, many families are obliged to be separate, even if they live outside the officially designated evacuation area, to look for some place where they can raise their children more safely. Many children in the region have gotten advice to not play outside either at school or in their neighborhood. Many animals, likes horses, cattle, pigs, chickens and pet animals, were left behind during the urgent evacuation. Many of them died of starvation or survive today in the wild. At best, the livestock was sold off at the lowest price.

Economic and community activities have shrunk or slowed down in the areas hit by the tsunami, and many people have lost stable jobs. However, even though people have started to resume step by step their economic activities in the Northeast, in the area victimized by nuclear fallout, there is no hope to start again their economic activities. Farmers, stock raisers, and fishermen have been obliged to leave their livelihood work. For generations, they have assiduously maintained fertile land, farm, and sea. However, radioactive materials now contaminate the environment. Producers outside the 30 km warned and 20 km no-admittance area also suffer from rumors that the products of Fukushima and the Northeast region in general are contaminated, even if scientific examination has shown that the products are safe. Several farmers who specialized in organic farming in the region have committed suicide from despair.

Food, even if it was produced outside the evacuation area, is often contaminated. When this situation occurs, the whole region where the contamination is reported is suspended to export the same sort of product. Beef and milk are often contaminated, because the cattle have eaten grass or feed coming from the contaminated region. From the rice to the meat to the fish to the water, and even the cement used in construction materials, high degrees of radioactivity have been discovered. Now no one can absolutely be safe in this country. Thus, the victims of the disaster have become spread across prefectural and even national borders.

The entire nation will thus ultimately pay the costs of this disaster. The government and TEPCO, operator of the Fukushima nuclear facility, should stabilize the cracked reactors where melted fuel has been found, cooling it by reworking the cooling system, and ultimately shutting down damaged plants. In December 2011, the government declared that the temperature inside the nuclear plants was found to be below 100 degrees centigrade and thus stabilized. However, the complete shut down of the reactor will take years and years. The Chernobyl accident, which took place in 1986, is still causing contamination in the surrounding area. At the same time, in Japan, like in other countries, no one knows where nuclear waste, both high-level and low-level, should be disposed. Until shut down can be accomplished and even afterward, the nation will continue to pay the costs.

In Fukushima, radioactive contamination was caused mainly at the time of the explosion of the four containment buildings in the station. However, radioactive materials continue to be emitted from the plant, contaminating the air, soil, water, sea and causing a hazard to life systems in Japan and the whole planet. The decontamination of soil has started in Fukushima prefecture with the grounds of schools. It is an enormous task, and the problem of how to dispose of the contaminated soil is critical. For the moment, it is just being buried at the sight, giving people worry of further contamination of soil, water, and the environment surrounding them. Actually, the problem of the disposal of nuclear waste as well as of contaminated water used to cool nuclear fuel has been raised. When a displaced 15 year old girl from Namie-cho in Fukushima was allowed to return for two hours to her house, located 4 kms from the exploded nuclear plants, to pick up necessities in the silence of a ghost town, she was reported to have said: "We can come back to collect the rest, the memories, that is, if they ever let us return here again." My question is: Who are "they" here? The government, the "atomic village", or her memories? She was obliged to separate herself from her cherished memories at home. However, she does not know when she can meet her memories again, or if she ever can.

Confrontation of Oppositional Development Paradigms: Economic Growth versus Post-Economic Growth

After the 3/11 nuclear disaster, we see the rise and confrontation of two different types of development concepts. Two different groups have emerged in a confrontation over these paradigms: one between the central leadership and local communities and the other within the central leadership itself.

As pointed out earlier, the economic growth of Japan was promoted and commanded by the central authority of politicians-bureaucrats-business world. The localities accepted that leadership in exchange for subsidies injected from the center. These subsidies were mostly financed by the high savings of the nation—including those from localities—as well as the debt of the government—both central and local since the central government urged local governments to finance a certain portion of funded development projects[4], the latter having often financed them issuing local bonds. This is why as GDP grew, we saw plenty of big infrastructural projects everywhere in Japan together with accumulated debt owed both by the central and local governments. In this way, the localities were depending on the center. The conservative politics assumed by the Liberal Democratic Party (LDP) assured the cohesion of this interdependent, domestic political structure.

However, there have been times that the localities have revolted against this orthodoxy of development, electing "innovative" or "oppositional" governors at the prefecture level. These have been mostly the case in big urban centers, such as Tokyo, Osaka, Nagano, Chiba, Shiga, Okinawa, etc. The "deep" rural areas have not been touched by this urban trend, and the Northeast is no exception. A new tide has appeared in these past two decades, which we will look at shortly. In the Northeast, a traditional bastion of conservatives, it has appeared with the reconstruction plan formed by localities after the 3/11 disaster.

In August 2011, Fukushima Prefecture adopted the "Fukushima Vision on Reconstruction", and in November, the "Fukushima Action Plan" accompanied the former. The documents draw a vision of reconstruction for the sustainable development of the prefecture based

---

[4] This varies according to locality, but in most cases about half. In the case of Okinawa Prefecture and localities who have accepted nuclear energy plants, up to 90% of the projects were funded by the central government.

on recyclable natural energy. This is a radically different picture from preceding development plans adopted by this prefecture for many years, when finance was heavily dependent on the subsidies related to nuclear power plants. Fukushima Prefecture had already accepted two nuclear power facilities that have ten reactors in total. This new plan is in opposition to the development pattern imposed until today by the center. It has the intention of promoting sustainable development based on local energy and resources.

On the other hand, at the central level, the former Naoto Kan administration had wanted to bolster the recovering of the economy. Before the severe hit by the 3/11 disasters, the Japanese economy had already been hit by the world-wide financial crisis starting in the mid-2000s with the Subprime Mortgage Crisis, the Lehman Shock, and then the more recent rise of the yen value that has adversely affected exports and accelerated the exodus of domestic factories to neighboring Asian countries. What has been the solution proposed by the center and its leadership?

On the international level, the government has shown interest in joining in the international talks concerning the Trans-Pacific Partnership Agreement (TPP)—promoted by the U.S.A. and aiming at accelerating trade liberalization in the Pacific area. The Japanese government wants to benefit from such an enlarged free trade area to assure more share in the newly emerging big markets in Asia. On the domestic level, the government wants to promote the entrance of big food processing companies into the Northeast, emphasizing large-scale production and cost efficiency. This is to prepare for international competition that will become intense with the progress of free marketization under TPP. However, I immediately understand that this policy of the central government might conflict with localities that are heavily dependent on agricultural and marine products mainly produced by small and medium producers as well as cooperatives of individual farmers and fishermen.

The opposition of two different paradigms of development is now clear: one is related to territorial development based on endogenous initiatives and local resources, emphasizing the full employment of local people and the equitable distribution of resources; the other emphasizes accumulation of capital by large enterprises based on the merger and acquisition of smaller firms. The latter solution might strengthen the cost efficiency of the Japanese economy. If the latter option becomes prevalent, it is clear that there will be more intense competition among large and small-medium enterprises, cooperatives, and small producers. This competition will bring more bankruptcy and unemployment to local areas.

This opposition of paradigms is visible also at the center. The political change that took place in 2009 shows the conflict between the growth cult adherents and the people who are not satisfied with the growing social gaps, poverty, and unemployment that have become visible after the 1990s when globalization was introduced to the Japanese economy. That is why the Democratic Party of Japan (DPJ) advocated a "change of the government" and won the national elections of August 2009, overthrowing the Liberal Democratic Party (LDP)-Komeito coalition. Among the platforms of the DPJ, the following ones show the most visible difference with the LDP led coalition: "Emphasis on education rather than cement works"; "Promotion of the New Public Commons (NPC)"; and "Regional Sovereignty."

> "Emphasis on education rather than cement works" criticized the policy of the growth-oriented period, when the LDP government disbursed huge budgets for public works to bring prosperity to large construction companies and local economies. This policy had support from both the big companies and the localities, however, it did not create permanent job opportunities in local areas. The jobs created by public works are always temporary and depend on other public works projects. The nuclear power plants entered in this category of "public works", besides their strategic value for energy and rearmament policy. The platforms of the DPJ emphasized more formation around people rather than around big public works projects for the sake of spending policy. They forecast that Japan will need to create a knowledge intensive type of economy in order to prepare for sustainable development in the future. This is also the way to overcome the crucial ageing issue for this country.

"Promotion of the New Public Commons (NPC)" is related to governance issues. In the growth period, governance was monopolized, as we have already pointed out, by the coalition of politicians-bureaucrats-business world. People were considered "consumers" and not interested in the management of society. At worst, they were considered "voters" but never active "citizens". "New Public Commons" means the partnership of the public and private sectors, including NPOs, in conducting development projects. It aims at two strategies: 1) to realize smaller government, and 2) to promote the participation of civil society in the management of the country as well as localities.

"Regional Sovereignty" means the change in the power relations between the central government and localities. It emphasizes the realization of equal footing between the two. In this sense, it is different from decentralization, which indicates the transfer of certain competences and resources that the center holds to localities. That is why regional sovereignty supposes more autonomy of localities.

All these platforms were innovative ones. However, they had, in fact, been expected for decades by a certain part of Japanese society that has become awakened with the development of civil society. The DPJ explored the new mentalities of the Japanese that have increasingly become sensitive to the issues of accountability and social gaps in the progress of economic globalization.

When the DPJ took power, however, they experienced problems of accommodating with the existing power structure composed of the politicians-bureaucrats-business world. A certain part of the DPJ itself is composed of a faction who left this structure due to personal political interests. That is why, after a change of the government that had been longed for by many citizens and voters, the conflicts inside the party turned into an intra-party struggle. The DPJ has not been able to advance their policies through three years and three administrations (Hatoyama, Kan, and Noda) since taking power. Then, they were confronted with the 3/11 disasters.

Actually, on the central government level, there are opposing camps of the two different notions of development.[5] One inherits the major lines of the platforms established for the August 2009 election and advocates the fulfillment of the nation's life rather than economic growth per se. It seeks to enlarge domestic demand through the redistribution of income and reform of the social security system.[6] This line of thought advocates the abolition of nuclear power plants and the promotion of natural energy. The other line of argument supports the recovery of the Japanese economy through promoting exports to world markets especially in Asia and entering in the TPP scheme on the international level, while promoting mergers and acquisitions and cutting social expenditure costs on the domestic level. The Noda administration seems to lean to the latter, while making efforts in tax-social security reform.[7] The balance between these two oppositional paradigms is subtle and precarious. We do not know yet which one will prevail in the years to come in this time of difficulty for the Japanese economy. However, it is clear that we are in a transitional stage from the preceding growth oriented period to that of preparing for the coming period of a more matured stage of economy.

In this stage, we see the contrast of different notions of development: one appears between the center and localities, and the other between the post-economic growth school and the economic growth school. In both cases, there is a contrast in development notions: one emphasizing a resetting of economic growth of the top-down type conducted by the centralized coalition of politicians-bureaucrats-business world; the other is more keen towards social development

---

[5] The conflicts between two different paradigms of development inside the DPJ are well explained by a series of articles published in the *Asahi Shimbun* entitled: "Post Economic Growth or Economic Growth? *Edanomics* versus *Maeharanomics*", January 8-10, 2012. *Edanomics* means the economic philosophy advocated by ex-Cabinet Director Yukio Edano, while *Maeharanomics* advocated that supported by Seiji Maehara, Chairperson of the Council of Policy Studies. The former adheres to the post-economic growth school and the latter shows familiarity with the economic growth school. The theory of post-economic growth in Europe is explained by Latouche, 2010.

[6] By unifying the social security system that divides regular employees and the other categories of the nation, such as housewives or self-employed people who are largely disadvantaged in comparison of the former.

[7] The combined tax-social security reform that the Noda Cabinet proposed to the Diet in January 2012 can be called an eclectic plan. Prime Minister Noda intends to finance the increasing costs of social security by increasing the consumption tax to 10%, but the proposed plan does not indicate any solution to reduce the huge governmental deficit, as was promised by the DPJ platforms.

supported by regional autonomy and citizens' participation for a more sustainable type of development. In recent years, the former has reached a deadlock due to the world-wide depression and accumulated deficit of the government—the so-called "sovereignty crisis". However, the traditional leadership wants to revive it, connecting the Japanese economy to world-wide/region-wide free markets. The latter is supported by a rising civil society that is keen to the widening social gaps between the small number of rich and the mass of people, who feel uncertainty in their future. In this critical moment, the 3/11 disasters took place and have had a huge influence on the Japanese rediscovery of spiritual values in society. We will see, in the next section, how Buddhism could constitute one of these new values.

Rediscovering Spiritual Values: Towards a New World of Autonomy, Participation, and Conviviality

In Japan, every year, a Chinese character is chosen to represent the trend of the epoch. At the end of 2011, the character *kizuna*, meaning "ties" or "relations", was chosen to represent the year 2011.[8] In a time of disasters, people rediscovered the importance and necessity of human ties, such as family, neighborhood, or mutual help. *Kizuna* was chosen in contrast to the progressing isolation of individual life in this era of economic globalization. The experience of the disasters has shown the Japanese the importance of social and human ties in life. Many people in Japan feel that in order to assure job and economic vitality, economic growth will be needed. However, in an age of uncertainty, they may rely on social ties and mutual help. In other words, spiritual value for human beings is being rediscovered.

At the time of the big earthquake and tsunami, Buddhist temples and priests played important roles for providing evacuation centers and for caring for people who lost their families, relatives, and houses. Japanese Buddhism has been considered to be asleep during this long era of high economic growth. People have said, "Buddhism is for

---

[8] This event is organized by the Japanese Association of the Competence and Certification of Chinese Characters on the basis of public vote. *Kizuna* received 61,453 votes, while the 2010 Character for "hot" received 14,537. The leap in number of votes from 2010 to 2011 shows that many Japanese now are keen to manifest their interests by appealing to this particular Chinese character of *kizuna*.

funerals". In turn, the need for spiritual care was replaced by trying to increase income every year. For many people who dropped out from the old temple system, new Buddhist denominations such as Soka Gakkai, Rissho Koseikai, etc. provided support and a place of refuge. However, at the time of the disasters, we saw the clear revival of Buddhism for assisting people who suffered, both materially and spiritually.

In terms of material help, there were of course some temples that were hit and decimated by the tsunami. However, many temples are located on higher ground in these mountainous, coastal areas. They have wide precincts and open halls for ceremonies. These temples provided emergency refuge for people who lost their homes. They served as distribution centers for food and assistance materials. They also accepted the remains of people who died in the tsunami of unknown identity until the relatives could identify them. Some temples near the Fukushima #1 facility provided space for debris which might be contaminated by radioactivity that no one including the government would accept for storage.

In terms of spiritual care, many priests who are familiar with their local neighborhoods provided spiritual care to depressed people. Rev. Setonai Jakucho—a famous novelist who became a nun and is now 89 years old—maintains a temple in Miyagi Prefecture where it is reported that she organized more than three hundred comforting dharma talks many of them held in the open-air in six months from April to September for people who lost everything including their relatives. Of course, spiritual care can be provided by every religion, however, the Northeast part of Japan is well known for the strong devotion of the common people in the rural and fishing villages to local Buddhist temples. We can say that Buddhist temples assumed a vital role for emergency aid and spiritual care to these suffering people. We have seen plenty of examples of how these people, who got care, have recovered strength to develop self-reliance and the reconstruction work of tomorrow.

Buddhism, however, is not only for this emergency work. The Buddhist teachings can also provide a focal point of reflection for the on-going reconstruction work. We have seen that the Japanese are in a transitional period from an era of economic growth to one of post-economic growth. This transition will bring a re-appraisal of wealth and happiness. The notion of happiness always constitutes the central objective of people's lives. In the era of economic growth, it was common that, for everyone, happiness derived from increasing income and material wealth, represented by an abundance of consumer goods. However, Japan has entered into this transition period where people increasingly want spiritual value and fulfillment of life *(ikigai)*; things once ignored in the time of economic growth,

What are the components of these spiritual values? As we have seen in preceding sections, they are related to autonomy and participation. The Fukushima Reconstrutcion Vision showed it well. The platforms of the DPJ indicated these new values. These values are, of course, interrelated. When regional autonomy becomes a major objective of development, it should be assured by the inhabitants' initiative and participation. Mahatma Gandhi foresaw this for the future of independent and peaceful India, which excluded caste division and overcame colonial mentality. He advocated two wheels for this journey: autonomy *(swaraj)* and self-sufficiency *(swadesi)* (Gandhi, 1982).

This development notion corresponds also to the spirit of the Sarvodaya Sharamadana Movement for village reconstruction led by A.T. Ariyaratne in Sri Lanka (Ariyaratne, 1999). Sarvodaya—which means everyone stands by him/herself and awakens to the truth—is based on a Buddhist philosophy. It rejects dependency on greed and encourages a life of middle way (moderation) with self-esteem, compassion, and wisdom. Now, after the 3/11 disasters, the Buddhist notion of development can provide a good and appropriate reference for the Japanese who are in search of the way of post-economic growth.

Ven. P.A. Payutto, a leading scholar monk in Thailand, has interpreted the Thai word for development *pattana*—a transitive verb meaning "to develop from above"—as based on the human tendency toward *tanha* (grasping). *Pattana* increases material wealth, emphasizing efficiency and competition. At the same time, however, it proliferates an acquisitive mind[9], a widening gap between the rich and poor, poverty and human deprivation, deterioration of the environment, disintegration of family and community life; in short, all sorts of human sufferings. While *bhavana*—an intransitive verb meaning "to open up oneself to universal truth or enlightenment"—is based on *chanda*, which means

---

[9] John Maynard Keynes called it: "animal spirit".

right effort to abandon grasping and the will to find out the truth. In order to increase the good and abandon the bad, we have to convert our *tanha* into *chanda*. Thus, *bhavana* is based on autonomy and self-sufficiency, which is the Middle Way of life and knowing how to be fulfilled. This idea corresponds to E.F. Schumacher's advocacy for "small is beautiful" and "Buddhist economics" (Schumacher, 1974), which corresponds to a life style in the post-economic growth period.

Now, in Japan, we are facing the opposition of different types of development paradigms: one is based on the high accumulation of capital and high economic growth; the other aims at a more stationary and mature type of economy that emphasizes the sustainability of society and environment. If we continue to seek after the high accumulation of capital and high economic growth, it will result in trouble and conflicts around the globe and further deterioration of the environment characterized by constant and increasingly large scale disasters. Here, the Buddhist philosophy of autonomy and self-sufficiency might give light to our choice. It indicates the end of an individualistic value system that has forged the ideological basis for a modern world system characterized by the constant increase of production, the pursuit of a profit-oriented mind as well as consumption (greed), increasing waste and the accelerating deterioration of the human environment, and ultimately the increase in conflicts and war.

The other model shows the components of a post-Fukushima/post-Globalization development model that emphasizes more endogenous development[10] of local communities and people's participation in them. People should find out their own meaning of life *(ikigai)* through the realization of a more non-violent *(ahimsa)* and sustainable type of development. In such a new phase of social development, based on the fulfillment of basic needs, the development of spirituality in a mutually caring community life will be crucial. This is one step towards a more convivial and peaceful world, as Ivan Illich once wrote (Illich, 1973). The Buddhist philosophy of development would support a direction towards a new page of the post-economic growth history of humanity. This is also an opportunity for the revival of Buddhism in Japan.

---

[10] Here, "endogenous development" means that one is autonomous *(swaraj; sarvodaya)* in the face of the impact exercised by the center and material civilization and that one follows only one's inner voice and one's community who perceives a spiritual correspondence with nature and humanity.

Conclusion:
The Role of Buddhism in the Transition of Japan from the Growth–Oriented Era to the Post-Growth Era

In this chapter, we have seen that the Fukushima nuclear disaster was the consequence of a development policy based on high capital accumulation and high waste, promoted by the centralized power structure of the country. The "developmentalism" of the power elite forged an economic structure aiming at high economic growth. The structure has been characterized by an international and domestic division of labor that emphasized efficiency and a high concentration of capital at the center. Its ethics are based on the endless acquisition of material wealth, domination over nature, and the discharge of huge wastes in it. It has caused social splits and endless environmental deterioration. The development of nuclear energy in the national provision plan of basic energy constituted an indispensable part of this particular growth-oriented structure. It led to an unstable and violent world characterized by the war of terrorism and counter terrorism as well as environmental deterioration that has caused many disasters. This type of development has brought and enlarged the world of death in our society, signaled by the Fukushima disaster.

Now after the Three Mile Island and Chernobyl nuclear disasters, the Fukushima nuclear disaster announces the end of "developmentalism" from above and of aiming at high economic growth. We are faced with moving ourselves to a world of post-economic growth, post-developmentalism, and post-economic globalization. This corresponds also to a world of sustainable development, as the Fukushima Reconstruction Vision suggests. There are emerging peoples and communities who aim at more autonomous and sustainable life styles and emphasize more socially oriented development and spiritually fulfilled lives. However, there are always people who believe in the merit of economic growth through creating jobs and material affluence, while the major factors for it have clearly been exhausted in the countries of the North.[11]

People nowadays are more concerned with spiritual values. It is time that we reconsider the treasure of human wisdom, including Buddhist philosophy. After the 3/11 disasters, there are good signs for

---

[11] aging population, smaller workforce, capital outflows, increasing costs, governmental budget deficits, etc.

the revalorizing of the teaching of the Buddha, such as the personal attainment of universal truth, a moderate lifestyle and knowledge of self-sufficiency, an understanding of causality through dependent origination, and conservation of the environment through an ethic of non-violence. When we abandon the value system that has forged the basis of the modern world—the endless pursuit of profit, the acquisitive mind, material affluence, domination over nature—the Buddhist philosophy will provide a good reference for this intellectual quest for an alternative.

Further, the validity of Buddhist caring was shown at the tragic time of the earthquake and tsunami in the Northeast. The All Japan Buddhist Federation declared in December 2011 the necessity of abolishing all nuclear power plants in the country. In this way, Buddhism can be relevant to the crucial choice of Japanese society, which is, "How will she escape from the growth-oriented stage and proceed to a post-growth, post-developmentalist and matured age?" This new period will be characterized by regional autonomy, endogenous development, reconstruction of communities once divided by globalization, mutual care and convivial life, concern with moderate lifestyles, environmental conservation, and concern with the fulfillment of spirituality in life. These new values are actually being sought by many Japanese, even if we do not call them Buddhist.

References

Ariyaratne, A.T. *Buddhist Economics in Practice in the Sarvodaya Shramadana Movement in Sri Lanka* (United Kingdom: Sarvodaya Support Group UK, 1999).

Gandhi, Mahatma. *Selected Works* (New Delhi, 1982).

Illich, Ivan. *The Tools of Conviviality* (London: Marion Boyars Publishers Ltd, 1973)

Latouche, *Serge. Farewell to Growth* (United Kingdom: Polity, 2010).

Payutto, Phra. *Buddhadhamma: Natural Laws and Values for Life* (Albany: State University of New York Press, 1995).

Payutto, Phra. *Buddhist Economics: A Middle Way to the Market Place* (India: Torchlight Publishing, 1996)

Schmacher, E.F. *Small is Beautiful* (New York: Harper Perennial, 1974)

A Priest's Work Amidst the Nuclear Ginza: A Profile of Rev. Tetsuen Nakajima

by Mai Ishikawa

The documentary film *Nuclear Ginza* (1995) introduces viewers to radioactive poisoned workers in the Wakasa Bay, Fukui Prefecture on the Japan Sea coast. The area has been dubbed "The Nuclear Ginza" for the 15 nuclear power plants lined up in a row like boutique shops in the cosmopolitan Ginza district of Tokyo. *Nuclear Ginza* shows the harsh reality that many workers at nuclear power plants suffer from, especially health problems caused by radioactive poisoning. The film also introduces a Buddhist priest, Rev. Tetsuen Nakajima, who has spent years appealing for awareness of the situation of nuclear power plants.

Rev. Nakajima is the chief priest of Myotsu-ji, a Shingon denomination temple located in Obama City in Fukui. Myotsu-ji is right in the middle of this region that hosts 15 out of Japan's 54 nuclear power reactors. This situation has led Rev. Nakajima to face the reality of the radioactive poisoned workers. He explains that there are various things that motivated him in his work amidst the Nuclear Ginza. "Most electricity is consumed in the cities. But the nuclear power stations are built in remote regions. My Myoutsu-ji temple is situated above the Nuclear Ginza on the Wakasa cost. There are 15 reactors here. Living up here, I couldn't go through life ignoring this issue."

The biggest event that moved him to get involved was meeting radioactive poisoned workers. "Meeting with radioactive poisoned workers and listening to their experience changed my life. I first met them when I was a university student at Tokyo National University of Fine Arts and Music. Before meeting them I was not interested at all in doing social work. However, I was moved by listening to how they have suffered. They suffer from various health problems. In addition, they are mentally damaged by prejudice and misunderstanding." Since meeting nuclear contaminated workers, he has worked on informing the public of the dangers of nuclear power.

He points out his religious background has also affected his motivation for anti-nuclear activism. He feels the importance of teaching of "the fully perfected virtue of benefiting oneself and others" *(niri-enman)*. A buddha perfects both self benefit *(jiri)* and other-benefit *(tari)*. Rev Nakashima thus explains that it is not about sacrifice, but rather the true way of harmonizing these two virtues. In terms of the nuclear problem, he says this idea can be applied in that all living things, including nature, are "others". Everyone is affected by others. In this way, the world would be a disaster if we all competed for our own self-benefit. The benefit and responsibility of nuclear power plants rely on the balance of "self-benefit" and "other-benefit".

In 1966, at the age of 24, Rev. Nakajima went back to his home town of Obama and started working as the vice abbot of Myotsu-ji. Along with helping out at the temple, he devoted much of his time to supporting the radioactive poisoned workers. First, he cooperated with other priests from different sects to do fact-finding research by listening to various workers from the nuclear power plants. In 1968, he started going on alms twice a month in his local village. He knocked on doors of nearby houses, rang a bell, and recited the mantra of Vairocana Buddha known as the *komyo-shingon*. He also handed out *Suzukoe*, a newsletter on religious topics and nuclear problems.

Since 1968, there have been continual plans to build new nuclear power plants in Obama. Rev. Nakajima encouraged local Obama citizens to say "No" to these plans and became a leading member of the Obama Citizen's Association Against Nuclear Proliferation to cooperate in the anti-nuclear power plant movement in Obama. He notes: "Most of the electricity is consumed in large, urban cities. However, nuclear power plants are built in depopulated areas. It costs a large amount of money to send electricity to urban cities. If the nuclear power plants are as safe as the electric companies say, then why don't they build them near urban cities?" Rev. Nakajima has felt that encouraging citizens is important to stop nuclear power plants from being built. It is the citizens who can vote "No".

However, he explains the difficulty in doing this work is that anti-nuclear activists tend to become isolated. This is because there are many local citizens who come to work for the electric companies or perform jobs related to the nuclear power plants. There is a wide network of subcontracted companies related to the nearby nuclear power plants. Therefore, many cannot speak their opinions publicly. He calls this situation in which people cannot speak their opinions on nuclear power plants "Nuclear Fascism".

He also explains that the city's autonomy is endangered by large amounts of government subsidies to build these nuclear power plants. "It is true that some in Wakasa have received subsidies for building nuclear power plants which has enriched them … However, once they are built it costs at least 10 million yen to maintain them." He claims this structural system has not changed from the 1980s.

Rev. Nakajima feels that the situation has not changed much from when the film *Nuclear Ginza* was made. He said the number of recorded people with radioactive poisoning has increased to 450,000 people. He also states that, "Although technology has improved, the problem of the workers still remains. The situation of radioactive poisoned workers still is critical, because the nuclear power plants are becoming older. The older the power plants become, the higher the level of radioactive pollution. Even now, 60,000 laborers work at nuclear power plants. Most of them are released and abandoned after two or three years."

In the early 1980s, he helped to found the country's first union for day workers at nuclear plants. The union made 19 demands of plant operators, including urging operators not to forge radiation exposure records and not to force workers to lie to government inspectors about safety procedures. Although more than 180 workers belonged to the union, its leaders were soon visited by thugs who kicked down their doors and threatened to harm their families. Rev. Nakajima notes, "They were not allowed to speak up. Once you enter a nuclear power plant, everything's a secret."[1]

However, there are times when he feels that his work in Obama is paying off. For example, when plans for a nuclear power plant in Obama came about twice in the 1970s, citizens cooperated in collecting

[1] Tabuchi, Hiroko. "Japanese Workers Braved Radiation for a Temp Job." *The New York Times*. April 9, 2011.

signatures. Also, recently in 2004 and 2008, Obama citizens voted for a city mayor that promised not to build a storage facility for nuclear waste in Obama. Therefore, the awareness concerning nuclear power has become very high in Obama.

In 1993, Rev. Nakajima helped to create the Inter Faith Forum for Review of National Nuclear Policy. This forum has gathered religious professionals—including Christians and Buddhists from other sects—from various places to network on anti-nuclear activities. Its main purpose has been to rethink the political background of Japan's nuclear policy. About the Forum, Rev. Nakajima says, "As a religious professional, I feel there is a great danger with the plutonium policy the government is trying to promote. To save the lives of our descendants, we have overcome sects and beliefs." Since the earthquake, tsunami, and subsequent nuclear disaster of March 11, 2011, the Forum has provided emergency evacuation housing in temples and churches for children and pregnant mothers in the areas around the Fukushima nuclear power plants.

The reality and danger of nuclear power plants were not well known to the Japanese public people until the March disasters. Especially, people in urban cities did not know the dark side of nuclear power plants. This is partially because the large electric companies have vast amounts of money to promote the "safety" and "necessity" of nuclear power plants. The public has been trapped by the electric companies and by the government as well into the view that nuclear power plants will help reduce global warming and support Japan's lack of natural resources.

Amidst all his activities as a chief priest, Rev. Nakajima has given various lectures to raise awareness. Presently, he concentrates on writing the magazine *Hatopoppo*, published six times a year with a distribution of 900 copies—500 copies go to people outside of Fukui Prefecture. This magazine is usually 15-20 pages in length introducing news articles, opinions by various readers, Rev. Nakajima's views, and information concerning the nuclear power plant issue in Wakasa.[2]

Rev. Nakajima comments about the difficulty of anti-nuclear

---

[2] Rev. Nakajima published a book in Japanese in 1988 called *Three Mile Island, Chernobyl, and then Japan … From the Nuclear Ginza in Wakasa* (*sri-mairu, cherunobuiri, soshite nihon … genpatsu ginza, wakasa-kara*) Koun-sha Publishers, Tokyo.

activities: "At first, it was about not building nuclear power plants; then shutting down the nuclear power plants; then finding out about nuclear pollution, polluted workers, and accidents. Right now, we are forced to think about ways of preventing large nuclear plant accidents from happening." He has broadened his activities through the years, connecting with other religious activists. In addition, his interests have broadened to politics, economics, and technology. He states, "Although my work is tiresome and may not have much effect, I want to keep spreading information and maintaining the anti-nuclear power movement for future generations." His background and motivation from a Buddhist point of view also continues to support his work. He believes now is the time for everyone—whether or not they are Buddhist—to take action based on the Buddha's words: "Do not harm sentient beings. Also, do not kill. And do not allow others to kill."

Inter Faith Forum for the Review of National Nuclear Policy

Emergency Appeal March 13, 2011

To the Prime Minister of Japan, Mr. Naoto Kan

In the face of this unprecedented crisis, we would like to thank Prime Minister Kan for showing your great determination and giving your message calling on all us citizens of Japan for determination in uniting as one. Despite the little that we ourselves can do, we will do our best in working to save the nation.

In this way, we have one proposal to offer:

At the Fukushima #1 nuclear facility, the #3 reactor that contains MOX—a mix of uranium and plutonium fuels—certainly appears to be in a grave situation, like the #1 reactor, of having an explosion in its building and emitting radiation.[1] If the containment vessel for the fuel is damaged by an explosion and a meltdown ensues, a very grave disaster will occur. Even if sea water is injected into the vessel, the water level will continue to go down. If the fuel rods are then exposed, the situation will become severe. It would not be a mistake to use *the strong pumps used by the United States military on its nuclear powered aircraft carriers to inject coolants or cold water into vessels on board. We would like to call on you to request the United States military to make an emergency mobilization for this purpose*—simply, as a last chance, special emergency matter. We would like to add to our request similar such measures for the #3 reactor at the Fukushima #2 nuclear facility.

Representatives of the Inter Faith Forum for the Review of National Nuclear Policy:

Rev. Tsutomu Shoji (United Church of Christ in Japan)
Rev. Hiroaki Osada (Jodo Shin Otani Pure Land Buddhist Denomination)

---

[1] A scenario that did indeed take place on the next day, March 14th.

Rev. Takumi Okayama (Jodo Shin Otani Pure Land Buddhist Denomination)
Rev. Shingo Naito (Japan Evangelical Lutheran Church)
Rev. Hidehito Okochi (Jodo Pure Land Buddhist Denomination)

April 10, 2011

Offer for Mid- and Long-term Evacuation to Safer Areas for connecting from a nuclear disaster to a future that protects life

There is a need for evacuating to safer areas for a period of 3 months children, those who are not yet adults, and pregnant women. Specifically, there will be an influence on children's health for the next 20 years, and we are concerned about the danger of exposure to radioactivity within their bodies. Thus, we have been thinking that as radioactivity is continuing to emit from the Fukushima reactors, there is a need to evacuate for 3 months to safer areas until the situation calms down.

In the case of adults, one should carefully observe one's condition and any effects for a month. According to the Japanese government's "Law Relating to the Prevention of Radioactive Injury by Plutonium Radiation", in cases in which exposure of 1.3 milli-sieverts over 3 months can be exceeded, then a radioactive boundary should be established. If you convert this figure to the short term, it comes to 0.6 micro-sieverts per hour. According to instructions, if you have been exposed to 0.6 micro-sieverts per hour of radioactivity in the atmosphere for over one month, then it is best to find an evacuation place.

Since 1993 we have been organizing a network of approximately 800 religious professionals—Buddhist, Christian, Shinto and others— from all over the country. In the face of the nuclear disaster at Fukushima, we are offering evacuation and lodging for up to 3 months for children and pregnant women.

We feel very strongly that there has not be a sufficient taking of responsibility to respond to the expanded incident and subsequent danger. Since the beginning of our network, we have brought forth formal complaints about the dangers of various aspects of nuclear power plants, such as its susceptibility to tsunamis and so forth, and predicted the kind of current situation we are in. However, we strongly regret that we could not mobilize local governments and businesses to work on this issue and to persuade citizens to foresee the kind of serious damage that can be caused by nuclear plants in order to avoid the disaster this time.

There needs to be different measures taken for evacuees than in accidents in the past. The earthquake, tsunami, and then nuclear accidents that followed one another in Fukushima constitute a nuclear disaster. This is of an entirely different nature from a singular natural disaster. It will not be fundamentally resolved by extending the measures towards disasters that we have experienced in the past. We need to move as far away as possible from the nuclear radiation zone.

Due to the unclear information at present, we have judged from our position as religious professionals that it is necessary to offer evacuation to the people in the disaster areas. While there is government and mass media information, there is also a lot of information circulating about on the internet that comes from domestic and international sources. It is a very difficult situation to see through to the reality when the information one wants is not readily available on one hand, and one then falls into the chaos of a deluge of information on the other. In this way, from the basis of the respect for life, we, as religious professionals deeply confronting the problem of nuclear power and exposure and illness from nuclear radiation, have judged that it is necessary to offer evacuation services to people in the disaster areas.

There is the possibility of using the homes or facilities prepared by our network. While we are offering evacuation services, the circumstances of each household are of course different. Buddhist and Christian priests involved in the network will make efforts to overcome these difficulties together through counseling with individuals. We have put on our homepage information on at least 30 such places. Further, the Jodo Shin Otani Pure Land denomination and the Japan Baptist Convention are both offering their temples and churches all over Japan to those in need.

Please consider a period of evacuation of 3 months. There can be a consultation if extended time is needed. To insure the safety of your evacuation, please inform us thoroughly of your future living plans. In the actual evacuation process, we will have the cooperation of the

Kansai volunteer group Re-Birth Japan. Please be patient with our administration as this is a relief operation.

Please use the following flow chart. This chart is not to be used for inciting anxiety amongst disaster victims. We have created it as a resource for making level-headed judgments on the reality of safe living.

1) In your family, do you have children who have not yet entered school or women who are pregnant?

    a) If NO → In your family is there anyone who is not yet an adult (19 years old)

    b) If NO → In your region or area has there been nuclear radiation in the atmosphere of 0.6 micro-sieverts per hour continuing for over a month?

    c) If NO → please monitor any changes from now on

If YES to 1a) or 1b) → A nuclear disaster is different from other disasters. Please exchange and share information → contact us

If YES to 1) → Do you have parents or close relatives who live at least 300 kms away?

If NO → Are you looking for a place to evacuate to? If YES → contact us

If YES → Do you need consultation about evacuating? If YES → contact us

Please contact us at your convenience!

Inter Faith Forum for the Review of National Nuclear Policy

Fukushima Office: Kosho-ji Temple (Jodo Shin Otani Pure Land Denomination)

Tel: 0242-83-2770

Tokyo Office: Juko-in Temple (Jodo Pure Land Denomination)

Tel: 03-3651-3175

e-mail: hit@nam-mind.jp

url: http://gts.mukakumuhei.net/

Questioning the Nuclear Accident: The Future and Religion

*I*n June 2011, the Bukkyo (Buddhist) Times *began a seven-week series of front-page editorials by Buddhists long involved in the nuclear issue in Japan. While Buddhists throughout the country were still busy attending to the victims of the tsunami and trying to avoid the ongoing nuclear crisis, the Bukkyo Timese courageously brought the long marginalized voices of these Buddhist activists to the attention of the mainstream Buddhist world, which it serves as one of the two main non-sectarian Buddhist newspapers in Japan*

Series 1 (June 2)

Religious Activities that also Issuing Warnings
The 3 Structures of Discrimination:
Rural Regions, Nuclear Contaminated Work, Children

Rev. Tetsuen Nakajima

Tetsuen Nakajima was born in 1942. In 1968 he began doing alms rounds in order to raise awareness and support for workers poisoned by radiation while also engaging in the anti-nuclear movement. He is the abbot of Myotsu-ji, a Shingon Omuro Sect temple in Fukui Province.

Wakasa (in Fukui Prefecture where I am from) has come to be called "The Western Nuclear Ginza" because of the 15 nuclear power plants there. "The Eastern Nuclear Ginza" is Fukushima. Together, they have been in operation for 40 years and have become antiquated structures with a variety of accumulating problems. In Fukushima, a catastrophic disaster has occurred which I think is truly embarrassing. This is not a matter of little concern. What is Fukushima today is Wakasa tomorrow. There is an urgent need for the comprehensive inspection of all nuclear power plants, and the ones that pose a danger must be closed down. We must overcome the possibility across the country of a second and third Fukushima.

In nuclear power in Japan, there are three structures of discrimination. The first is the discrimination of cities towards the rural areas. Wakasa and Fukushima both send huge amounts of energy to cities. For example in 2008, the 11 reactors of the Kansai Electric Power Company (KEPCO) in Wakasa generated 62 billion kilowatts of electricity per year. Within Wakasa, we consumed 600 million kilowatts, a sum that does not even exceed 1% of this total. The meaning of commandeering under populated areas to produce nuclear power for urban areas is very clearly seen in these accidents. The "Myth of Safety" is a cover for the current location of these reactors.

The second structure is the problem of nuclear contaminated work. Over forty years, there have been a total of 450,000 people forced to work amidst nuclear contamination. Regulations on the over exposure to radiation have been routinely dismissed. Labor has been used and discarded in a structure of wretched subcontracting. In the management of the Fukushima accident, from 7,000 to 8,000 laborers have already been awash in radiation levels that exceed standards in desperate death defying work. These many sacrifices have foremost been to secure our present way of living. This is just like the suicide kamikaze pilots at the end of World War II.

The third structure is the vulnerable victims of the nuclear accident who are children. They have been exposed to levels of 20 milli-sieverts of per year, similar to the radioactive contaminated workers. For children with a future, this is a much more dire situation than for adults. There are 300,000 children up through the age of high school in Fukushima. As also in the case of Chernobyl, it is clear that children are more susceptible to radioactivity than compared to adults. As age lessens influence increases. Women who are pregnant as well as the young generation who will be born and raised will be greatly damaged. This is unforgiveable.

The great electrical power that was given birth to by nuclear generation has surely brought great prosperity to Japan. However, this brightness at the same time has a deep shadow that carries with it discrimination. This disaster affords us an opportunity we must take in order to subjugate it. Nuclear policy, which began as a national policy, has brought together a cast of giant construction firms, giant manufacturers, electrical companies, and compromised academics. In recent years, there has been a so-called nuclear renaissance around the world with the promotion of nuclear power in Asia and the Middle East. However, with the Fukushima disaster, there has been a cooling of the waters. Within this gigantic system, an ethical viewpoint is emerging from the stench of the failing nuclear administrative system as well as its antiquated culture. The wreckage of the Fukushima reactors reflects to our eye a symbolic image of this breakdown.

The Inter Faith Forum for the Review of National Nuclear Policy in Japan has investigated the history of nuclear development and developed an argument concerning the process of modernization. Japan's modernization began with the shock of Commodore Perry's "black ships" from the United States in 1854. Japan then proceeded to develop national slogans such as, "Quit Asia, Enter Europe", "Cultural Progress", "Rich Nation, Strong Military", and then sacrificed many precious lives in World War II. However, after the war, we continued on this path. I have spoken of the new tacit slogans "Quit Asia, Enter America", "Faith in Scientific Technique", and "Great Economic Nation". Large-scale production, large-scale consumption, and large-scale disposal, as personified in the giant nuclear power crowd, became an extension of the modernization process since the coming of the black ships. At all times, there has been the demand for quantification, speed and pleasure, and economism. This kind of awareness supported "The Myth of Need" at its roots. Now, we have to undergo a deep process of self-reflection.

Religious professionals have been performing memorial services for those who have died (since the triple disaster in March 11), and we must engrave in our hearts their heartbreaking sacrifice. A memorial service has the positive meaning of "not to forget". Still today, it is very important to get spiritually and emotionally intimate in order to save those people in dire straits. It is important to lodge formal complaints and bring to justice the administration of national and local governments. Then, in order not to repeat in the future this tragedy, we have one religious duty to disseminate information.

A vision towards the future is not about advantages that are easily seen. The things that are blessings and the way that one treasures life must be based in the standards of values. This is the practice of the Four Noble Truths: one ascertains the fundamental causes of the problem; one then resolves them; and one follows the causes that come from ideal results. We must connect to the truth of working together as well as developing a dialogue and common expressions to the various views of other people. The practice of the logic of the Four Noble Truths supports in a spirit of compassion the genuine demand for a blessed world. The meaning of blessed is not something that only religious people should be asking. Politicians and academics should also start a process that everyone must think about.

Shouldn't Infants Be Given Priority for Shelter? The Situation of the Weak Having Their Lives Exposed to Danger

Rev. Kanjo Umemori

---

*R*ev. *Kanjo Umemori is the abbot of Ho-un-ji, a Nichiren denomination temple in the tsunami hit region of Miyagi Prefecture. Born in 1956, he is a part-time researcher at the Nichiren Contemporary Research Institute. As a representative of the Inter Faith Forum for the Review of National Nuclear Policy, he has been participating in the anti-nuclear movement, pointing out the problems of the Japanese government's nuclear power policy, and presenting his views to the National Atomic Energy Commission.*

Some 20 years ago, with colleagues in the movement, we put up a signboard very near the Onagawa nuclear power plant in Miyagi Prefecture, which said, "In an accident, can it be shut down? Can we together shut it down?" To see that the sign is still there in good condition has only deepened my anger and vexation. In talking about my original purpose, if there had been a small accident previously, public opinion might have heightened and the ossified nuclear energy policy might have undergone some gradual change. This is something that I might have actually been hoping for.

However, the incident that did finally happen is where I live. I am only a little more than 100 kilometers from an accident so severe that it is on par with the scale of the Chernobyl accident. As we approach the three month mark since the disaster, a resolution can still not be seen. Radioactivity is still being continuously emitted into the atmosphere everyday. This is a kind of cruelty piled onto the situation that has already happened with the tsunami, to the point where we can't even remember when the catastrophe began.

For over 20 years, we have had the aim to ring alarm bells on this issue. In a booklet published in 1989, I wrote, "The Japanese archipelago is almost entirely a region of earthquakes. The nuclear power plants along the coasts are continually exposed to the dangers of earthquakes and tsunamis. Moreover, since the reactors are concentrated in one area, it is impossible not to think of the nightmare in which there are multiple meltdowns of their cores all at once." If there was a voice from heaven, it would have sent messages several times of the chance to turn back.

If we also look at the limits of Tokyo Electric Power Company (TEPCO), we see: the scandal in 2002 of the false reporting in a routine governmental inspection of its nuclear plants and the systematic concealment of plant safety incidents; in 2007 the dangerous situation of the Kashiwazaki-Kariwa nuclear power plants caused by the Chu-etsu earthquake in nearby Niigata Prefecture; and also last year in June 2010 the incident of the Fukushima #1 reactors almost losing power. It is impossible to say the incident in March was "beyond expectation" as the TEPCO authorities have done. We have been bracing ourselves for a while for this situation today.

After the disaster, I got telephone calls from friends and acquaintances from all over the country worrying about our safety saying things like, "The things that you continuously talked about have come true." Originally, in order to prevent this situation from happening, I lodged formal complaints about the dangers and explained a different course for basic national policy. However, my voice could not reach the government or businessmen, not to mention the common people.

The real severity of a nuclear disaster is difficult to express in spoken words. Can anyone condemn the relief vehicles that turned back at 20 to 30 kilometers from the plants? In the damage of the tsunami, the search for bodies and rescue was completely abandoned. At the time of the disaster, there were reports of impressive relief efforts being undertaken, but there were no reports from in front of the nuclear accident. Volunteer groups of supporters from the Nichiren denomination headquarters who piled relief goods into trucks and visited on their own could also be heard expressing anxiety about the radiation.

My knowledge of the fear of nuclear power starts from the nuclear meltdown incident at Three Mile Island in the United States that happened when I was graduating university in March 1979. I have clear memories of images of pregnant women and children rushing to evacuate. Because the building that housed the reactor near the Harrisburg Airport had thick walls, it narrowly escaped the kind of explosion that blew up the building at Fukushima. However, in the area around the plants at Three Mile Island, the soil contaminated by the radioacitivy sprouted giant sunflowers.

The incident at Fukushima this time is of the same type, but it is much more severe. Three of the reactors have melted down and a fourth has had a hydrogen explosion. Buildings have been destroyed exposing a pitiful structure that has created further trauma. This Level 7 incident continues to progress today.

The incident at Fukushima is beyond that of Three Mile Island, yet there is no evidence that pregnant women and small children were given priority for evacuation. During the initial stage, we also didn't hear of the wide distribution of iodine which blocks the contamination of a child's thyroid. This is because it had not been determined to be a severe disaster. In order to carry out the so-called duty of stopping widespread panic, the media and compromised academics have issued pathetic statements of "reassurance" that have made fools of the hearts of people who cling to this information and have resulted in a direct impact on the lives of the defenseless and weak.

Furthermore, the Ministry of Education, Culture, Sports, Science and Technology (MEXT) accepted an annual radiation level of 20 milli-sieverts for the schoolyards of Fukushima. I am filled with sorrow and shame with this country because it is not ashamed to accept a radioactive environment 20 times higher than a normal community, in which children are already several times more susceptible to radiation. In the critical incident at the Tokaimura nuclear plant in 1999, I knew the real situation of how the government did not protect the people, and I am shuddering that the slogan "Believe in Japan" has been used again to kill people.

In the Kamakura Era (1192-1333), Master Nichiren encountered great earthquakes and wrote the *Rissho Ankokuron* to admonish those who had endangered peace and slandered the true dharma. Amidst this, there were formal threats by other countries towards Japan, such as when the Mongols launched an invasion in the final years of this period. Nichiren suggested that the government had brought these natural and human disasters upon themselves. In this way, what does slandering of the true dharma mean in the present era?

Furthermore, why won't anyone point out the fact that the Buddha's home country of Shakya was destroyed? This may not be the right time to say this, but I feel sorrow for the deceased country of the Buddha that he himself tried three times to intervene to save. But the Buddha in his farsightedness saw that it was alright that the Shakya Kingdom should fall into ruin due to its previous bad karma, and so he remained silent from then on. A country that doesn't grasp for a renewed intention will otherwise come to ruin it seems. I think we can verify this.

It is profound that the 49th day anniversary of this disaster coincided with the anniversary of Nichiren founding our denomination on April 28th. In this way, we chant towards the morning sunrise over the Pacific Ocean that wrought the great tsunami and nuclear accident to raise awareness of the illumination to guide us to revival.

The Insecurity of Confronting the Antiquated Nuclear Power System: Towards the Next Generation of Energy in "Atmospheric-Pressure Plasma"

Tatsuhiko Yajima

---

*T*atsuhiko Yajima is a Professor of the Department of Life Science and Green Chemistry at the Saitama Institute of Technology, just north of Tokyo. Born in 1952, he specializes in environmental chemistry, plasma chemistry, and electrical chemistry. He is also participating in the planning of The Science and Buddhist Thought Research Center affiliated with the Saitama Institute of Technology's Institute of Advanced Science.

In order to realize a low carbon society that does not produce carbon dioxide emissions, the greater part of Japan's energy policy has over compensated towards nuclear energy. I would go so far as to say that until the Tohoku disaster this low carbon society model was endorsing nuclear power. There has been the plan to reduce carbon emissions by 25% by the year 2020 through the potential of increasing nuclear power. However, this policy was grounded in the myth of nuclear safety and is now being called entirely into question and reconsideration since the recent disaster.

Nuclear power has been considered an important energy source on the basis that it doesn't emit carbon dioxide, and this fact led it to become 40% of Japan's total energy supply. Other substitute or alternative energies such as thermal, water, solar, geo-thermal, wind, and wave energy don't even make up 10%. If nuclear energy were abolished in one shot, it is clear that domestic production activities could not be sustained, and the economy would fall into disorder.

Therefore, we will have to face the realistic policy of maintaining nuclear power while the development of new forms of energy proceeds during this momentary suspension of nuclear power facilities. Germany has already decided to abolish all nuclear energy by the year 2022, and there is the sudden, rapid advance of innovative techniques for natural energy, beginning with wind power. To the extent that Japan does not change course away from nuclear power, the development of new technologies will not proceed.

The re-thinking about the present nuclear crisis is that in reality nuclear power involves techniques with an extremely high level of cost. If we include the costs of compensating the victims of the nuclear disaster, there is absolutely no basis for making profit. The facilities needed to create giant amounts of energy tend to cause serious accidents and therefore need to be absolutely safe. To make 100% sure that such accidents don't happen requires an enormous cost.

The phrase "beyond expectation" has been repeatedly used in fallacious arguments by authorities to evade taking responsibility for the incident. There is no guarantee that a disaster beyond our estimations will absolutely no happen. It's not possible to fully estimate the future probability within the past framework. This is not an exaggeration. If we speak in terms of a disaster brought on by the power of nature, we might have the slightest possibility of estimating how to overcome it. The problem is that this incident was man made— through negligence and corruption—so there were absolutely not estimations made for such a scenario. None of the many ideas from hypothetical models for a course of action to get out of the worst situation could apply. In this situation today, there still lingers into the future the insecurity of how to cope with these antiquated nuclear facilities and equipment.

Public opinion for eradicating nuclear power has increased. Further, many companies have created their own stable sources of energy by installing their own in house electricity generation. There are many cases of the installation of liquefied natural gas (methane). Since methane is a chemical compound from one carbon, it can generate a large amount of heat and the emission of carbon dioxide from one unit of generated heat is half that of coal and 20% less than gasoline.

When nuclear power first became a main source of electrical energy, a big problem that emerged was the uneven distribution of it in rural regions. It has been a system of sending electricity to urban areas while generating it in the rural areas. From now on, there is the need for small and medium scale electrical resource facilities in each region. In this way, if one electrical source breaks down, then electricity can still be supplied without stoppages or planned blackouts. By converting to a decentralized supply system, electricity can be generated and consumed locally. In this case, citizen's business initiatives can get involved in electrical enterprises, while establishing competitive business principles.

If this were done on a massive national scale, like nuclear power, it would not be possible to develop electrical generating techniques that are high in safety. However, alternative energy resources, such as water and wind, presently offer insufficient amounts of electricity. At the same time, in order to burn fossil fuels, thermal power and large scale electrical generation emit high levels of carbon dioxide. In order to deal with this issue, thermal electrical generation needs to be cut in half in order to have techniques to develop a high number installations with high safety.

I myself am promoting research in "Eco-Process Chemistry" in which we can live in co-existence with the environment; for example, a system for the practical application of energy resources that uses "atmospheric-pressure plasma". The sequence of discharging energy from plasma can be done at a relatively low cost. Lightening and aurora are examples of the plasma phenomena in the natural world. Using the medium of carbon-felt, it is easy to generate atmospheric-pressurized plasma. If you put plastic into a plasma device to make gas, the gas can be used as a new chemical material. Even with the enthusiastic advance towards zero emission renewable resources, about 50% of the 10 million tons of annual disposable plastic is still disposed of by incineration; 16% is recycled; and the rest put in landfills. Further, there is the problem of the heat needed for this process that emits carbon dioxide and is a waste of resources. This problem, however, could be eradicated in one shot.

"Atmospheric-pressure plasma" is one idea for recovering electrical resources. Japan is an ocean nation. If we efficiently used the resources contained in the ocean, Japan would be a nation of resources— instead of being known as a resource poor nation. In the principle of electrical generation, a system of heating water into steam revolves a moving turbine. In nuclear energy and thermal energy, the source of heat is different, but the mechanism is the same. There is a material that can be used again and again for this source of heat and is contained in seawater. It can be extracted by the technique of "atmospheric-pressure plasma".

After the Fukushima nuclear disaster, there has begun around the world the all-out development of next generation energy. I myself am thinking of how to establish a new technique that incorporates the Buddhist concept of "interbeing" *(kyosei)*.

Let's Deeply Consider Things from the Side of Suffering: The State of Society Can be Changed

Rev. Hidehito Okochi

---

*R**ev. Hidehito Okochi was born in 1957. He is the abbot of Juko-in, a Jodo Pure Land temple in Edogawa Ward, Tokyo, where he helps run a variety of local NGOs focused on ecological living, community support, and activism in various social issues, such as the Palestine Children's Campaign and the Citizen's Network for Thinking about Global Warming.*

In commemorating the 800th anniversary of the death of its founder Honen this year, the Jodo Pure Land denomination created two themes to mark the event. The first is the shift of Kamakura Buddhism—of which Honen was one of the principal architects—to the side of the people through developing a faith based in the value of community. In this different age today, democracy has been as a virtue of contemporary society, yet I would like to ask, "Is it really the case that we have taken responsibility to ensure such a society?" The other theme is the vow to emancipate all life. Honen demonstrated through his encounters with both the warrior Kumagai Naozane and the prostitute at the port of Muro that life should never be thrown away. Rather, the deeper a person's failings are should lead us to help them all the more. From these two themes, I believe we should develop a way of thinking that is exactly opposite to nuclear power.

Concerning the theme of supporting all life, we can see that when nuclear power becomes operable, it is inevitable that radiation will eat away at the health and lives of sentient beings. The Inter Faith Forum for the Review of National Nuclear Policy to which I belong has been connecting with families who's loved ones have lost their health and even their lives as radioactive poisoned workers at the nuclear power plants. We have also turned our attention to the voices of parents with children who have shown congenital illnesses and/or illnesses connected to radioactive contamination like cancer to internal organs and leukemia. The very nature of nuclear power tolerates this kind of sacrifice and buries it in darkness.

The Trick of Nuclear Power

However, there is this continual insistence that we must have nuclear power in order to enjoy prosperity and convenience. In other words, our lifestyles require nuclear power—but is this really so? For myself, I thought that this is the trick, the problem of nuclear power at its root— that the democracy we first championed cannot advance under such influence. It is clear that living in this contemporary society, we use electricity extravagantly and surround ourselves with wasteful things. But in the end, the things that we buy and use are not really things we need, but rather have been designed for us to consume. We have been induced into using these things even though we don't need them. Until we investigate and interrogate this system, that is, changing the political and economic system, then the tragedies that hit the young will continue to be repeated. In the Buddhist discipline *(sila)*, it is worse to sell alcohol thank to drink it.

From the beginning, Japanese have been weak in facing the authorities, while maintaining a strong sense for regulations and rules. Now, our own lifestyles have been condemned, and we feel ashamed; but this diverts us from investigating the real structural problems. The result has been that many Japanese have given up thinking "deeply" for themselves and "taking responsibility for the final consequences".

A few days ago, I was invited as a panelist for a talk on thinking about the state of society at a university in Tokyo. When it was pointed out that there are very few students who have been participating in the anti-nuclear protests over the past months, one person said in response,

"I don't think there is much meaning in protesting. For myself, I'd rather do a candlelight vigil with friends and develop an attitude to saving electricity." Unfortunately, this sentiment is just what the promoters of nuclear power want. Certainly developing an attitude towards saving electricity is not bad, and it would be good to do on a large scale. However, the most important thing now is changing the way electricity is generated and delivered. This kind of thinking does not lead towards such a change, while it helps to conceal the suffering of people and prevents a deepening awareness of the problem.

Towards a Cyclical Society

The authorities have been denying the effects of the influence of radiation for years and have ordered the fraudulent recording of deaths about the laborers within the nuclear power plants and the residents in the area of the plants. The causes of death have been written down as "heart failure" though they died while they were fighting the effects of cancer and leukemia. In the area of Wakasa in Fukui Prefecture—which hosts the "Nuclear Ginza" of 15 reactors—patients were transferred to the Kansai Electric Power Company Hospital in Osaka so that their true conditions could be hidden. A few people fought this, but most have been buried in darkness. It is the role of religious professionals to discern the true reality by experiencing the ground level where people are thrown away. Then, they should present a way of living and a way that society should be.

For the past 20 years, some residents from my area of Edogawa Ward in Tokyo and I have visited the locations of where waste from dams and nuclear power plants are dealt with. Listening to the local people who have been forced to suffer for the comforts of our present society, we came to think this is "the place" where society and nature are destroyed. Therefore, I think that we must do some kind of activity, somehow, that leads to self-awareness and personal responsibility towards where one lives as "the place" for determining consumption patterns and policy making. Starting with the real situation of electricity, we should thoroughly clarify the mechanism of the financial system. This begins by examining the system of gross cost as well as the government financing system. With the goal of a "non-nuclear, low carbon society", we can combine a loan financing system with clean energy. From the maintenance of social capital at the community level, we can present the model of a cyclical society—in which production, consumption, and waste feedback into each other. This should be something that we should all feel is within reach.

However, we must now bear the burden of the suffering of radioactivity that will last for some decades or even centuries. This is an irreparable situation that will effect our children and grandchildren, but we must now become intimate with the tragedy and squeeze out as much positive energy as we can to link to the future. I think this is the mission of those who are living now to truly make a common connection between the past and future. In order to realize a "true society", it will require the utmost commitment to serving society. Together with the silent victims, we are working to recover hope for 300 years into the future.

Towards a Nation Founded on Natural Energy: Religion Has a Role in Controlling Greed

Mutsuji Yamaoka

---

*M*utsuji Yamaoka is the head of Public Relations and Publishing for the Japanese religious group Seicho-no-Ie. Born in 1955, he also serves as the Director of the Religious Researchers Eco-Initiative, a new organization working cooperatively on preservation of the global environment.

Still today we are being taught the lesson of the suffering of trying to control the radiation emitting from the Tokyo Electric Power Company's Fukushima #1 nuclear facility. What is it that this "The Future and Religion" Series is asking about this incident? If we can speak of a conclusion or judgment, in terms of the future, it must be the decision to shift from the present Japan dependent on nuclear power to "a nation founded on natural energy". In this way, Seicho-no-Ie is working to achieve the role of confronting human greed, which is a shared teaching of all religions. At the same time, we think it is important to show how to realize a society that harmonizes nature and humanity.

In what way then should we think about nuclear energy? The President of Seicho-no-Ie, Masanobu Taniguchi, wrote an article entitled "Is a 'Nation Founded on Nuclear Power' OK?", which appeared in his blog, "Lots of Thoughts in a Short Space" on June 24, 2006. In three points, he clearly shows that that we cannot endorse "The Plan for a Nation Founded on Nuclear Power" in which the National Agency of Natural Resources and Energy and the Ministry of Economy, Trade, and Industry (METI) would be combined. The first point states that nuclear energy does not fit with "the realization of a cyclical society (of production and consumption)", an idea generated by the reflection on global warming. The second point calls for respect for intergenerational equity, which gives way to the third point, the realization of a decentralized society using natural energy. Nuclear energy is at odds with all of these points.

First of all, the fuel used in nuclear power cannot be said to be cyclical in nature. The fuel that is finished being used from all the nuclear reactors in Japan is about 1,000 tons annually. This used fuel is put into storage pools within nuclear reactors or in storage pools at reprocessing sites located in the huge Rokkashomura complex in northern Aomori Prefecture. After some years, these storage pools become filled to the brim. The final storage facilities for this fuel have also become full and additional facilities have not been decided upon. In this way, we see that a society that depends on nuclear power is absolutely not a cyclical one.

So what about intergenerational equity? For the time being, we must quickly shut down the nuclear power plants and store the approximately 16,000 tons of used nuclear fuel sitting in pools in places that will not bring harm to humans. It is said that to pay the price for reprocessing nuclear waste will take 10,000 years and span across generations. In this way, nuclear power goes against intergenerational equity. This sort of nuclear problem has revealed the physical dangers to the citizens in the surrounding areas, and so the decision to get rid of reliance on nuclear power is the most basic choice to be in accord with intergenerational equity.

If we adopt the viewpoint of realizing a cyclical society that uses natural energy, nuclear power based on a large-scale centralized system cannot work. The problem then becomes reforming the structural monopoly over the production and delivery of energy by the electric companies. If we can realize the division of production and delivery throughout the country, we will be able to promote the full-scale use of natural energy, such as wind and solar, that is in tune with different localities.

In 2001, Seicho-no-Ie acquired ISO14001 certification, which establishes standards, guidelines, and policies governing correct environmental management. In this way, we are not only trying to reduce the consumption of energy by each center, but we also are producing natural energy through the active promotion of the installation of solar generation equipment. The result has been that for 863 members in 712 work places we have installed solar panels that have generated a total of more than 5,253.45 kW.

We have also decided that by the Spring of 2013 we will move our headquarters, presently located in Shinjuku in downtown Tokyo, out to "an office in the forest" located in Yatsugatake-nanryo in Hokuto City in Yamanashi Prefecture, near Mt. Fuji. In this plan, we will begin to deal with the long-term process of the nuclear problem by creating energy from solar and biomass and making ourselves self-sufficient. The completion of such an office we think will offer one model of a society based in cyclical natural energy.

However, can we say that the large-scale production of cyclical natural energy will match the amount of energy produced by existing nuclear energy? Absolutely not. Our present society expects that we will once again promote a lifestyle that pushes forward with prioritizing greed and the destruction of the natural environment. However, religion originally seeks to hold down human greed and speaks of a way of living that has gratitude for the blessings of heaven and earth that have been granted to us. If this is so, I think that religion has an important role in spreading the idea of human happiness through a lifestyle of gratitude and the control of human greed—and this points towards a nation founded upon natural energy.

We must now practice the Four Divine Abodes of Buddhism (*brahmavihara:* the mind of loving kindness, compassion, sympathetic joy, and equanimity) not just for fellow humans but for the natural world. The move of our office to the forest will also add to the meaning of the practice of the fourth *brahmavihara* of equanimity by cutting off from the attachment to materialistic greed that "big city society" continues to awaken in humans. At our new offices, I think that humanity and nature will be harmonized and that we will be able to learn directly from the Yatsugatake-nanryo forest and experience a mentally luminous lifestyle with a low carbon footprint. These are the practical responses by Seicho-no-Ie to the question of the future after the nuclear incident.

Driving the Ecosystem towards Malfunction: Emergency Evacuation for Pregnant Women and Children

Taeko Kansha

---

*T*aeko Kansha is the temple wife of Ryukoku-ji, a Soto Zen temple in Fukushima. Born in 1946 in Fukushima Prefecture, she is the author of "It's still not too late – the longest letter I have ever written", published by Jiyusha. She now resides in Fukuoka Prefecture.

The incident at the Fukushima #1 nuclear facility was something, contrary to what the authorities said, actually "within expectation". Up to this moment, the electric companies and the nation completely disregarded and turned a deaf ear to warnings pointing out such a scenario.

Twenty-five years earlier, when the Chernobyl nuclear incident occurred in the former Soviet Union, the radiation emitted from an explosion and fire at a reactor crossed national borders and even beyond Europe to include all of the northern hemisphere. Food in every country, even beyond the former Soviet Union, was contaminated, and every country was forced to develop measures to deal with the situation. Citizens were not able to get daily food that had not been contaminated by the widespread radiation. Babies, unborn fetuses, and children who had been exposed to internal radiation came down with leukemia and thyroid cancer some years later, and one after another, the lives of the young were deprived. The 135,000 citizens who lived within a 30-kilometer radius of the reactor were forced to evacuate, and still now, no one can live in this area. In Fukushima, there is a village named Aka-uki, also known as Nami-e Machi, where radiation was detected that was three times the amount of Chernobyl's boundary of forced evacuation.

I was shocked when I heard a talk on the Chernobyl incident in 1986, so I began to read books about related issues. The more I searched, the more I saw a lack of logical consistency, and I began to freeze up in fear. In general, we are not informed about these facts and reality. The situation is one of being inundated by a steady stream of nothing but one-sided "myths of safety and necessity". In this way, I wrote a letter out of desperation called, "It's still not too late – the longest letter I have ever written", which was published by Jiyusha Books. By word of mouth, I received a lot of sympathy from people who had read it, and unbelievably, it sold 500,000 copies through wide circulation. Many of the readers were mothers who had children.

The reason I think the popular protests today say we "don't need" nuclear power or that "it shouldn't exist" is because it is inimical to life. Radiation and life force cannot co-exist. Local ecosystems malfunction, and life force collapses. We have inherited a continuous line of life force of 3.6 billion years. This life force is passed through our genes in cells one by one, which are even up to today still evolving. However, radiation damages and alters these genes and blots out life force, which collapses before long. This radiation coming from nuclear power generation has been created in massive amounts, and humans cannot handle by hand the eradication of this poison. In this world of so much life force, humans are given life and sustained. This is not a concept but a reality. In this way, we must have the vow that human existence should be above politics, economics, and culture. We cannot mistake the means of human economic activity for the end of human safety.

Nuclear power is first generated by the process of the fission of uranium within a reactor. An intense heat is created that boils water and the ensuing steam turns a turbine that creates electricity. In short, water is brought to a boil through a nuclear reaction, but natural gas, coal, and oil can accomplish the same goal. The need for uranium surely involves radioactive materials. This requires complicated techniques that involve "stopping a fission process", "cooling a reactor core", and "confining the radiation". The accompanying facilities are hugely complicated. This nuclear process and its facilities end up costing an immeasurable amount of money.

In this method of generating electricity, which in its complexity goes beyond being dangerous, 2/3 of the heat energy becomes thermal effluent and is futily dumped into the ocean. Within this thermal effluent, there are chemical substances and radioactivity.

Simply, in order to bring water to a boil, we have used a fuel that emits deadly poisonous radioactive materials. We must face the warning of this preposterous danger. It is too late to return to the way it was before. It makes me fearful to think about near future.

This time it has gradually become clear that the nuclear power industry is made up of politicians, bureaucrats, big business, the electrical power companies, and scholars with their nest of vested interests. The truly disappointing part is that the mass media has been co-opted into this agenda to carry out a role. Most people still do not know the serious truth of nuclear power. People don't realize how ignorant they are.

What is worse than this is what nuclear power has created: a massively high level of radioactive waste that is coming in contact with our human environment and that we will have to continue to deal with for the next one million years, as reported by the U.S. government in February of 2009. In this time period, there will be certainly large earthquakes and other disasters. How in the world will anyone alive today take responsibility for this? Isn't this a crime committed on the next generations? Shall we allow a method of generating electricity that requires in exchange the lives of others and threatens life force?

If we are to overcome the incident that happened this time, we must deal with the radiation that has been scattered over a wide area and the contamination of air, water, land, humans, animals, and vegetables. We have been completely robbed of our lifestyles. After the incident, the restoring of high quality food standards is ongoing, and there is special concern that radioactive poisoned victims among children will appear. Have we come to an awareness that this country is experiencing the karmic retribution of nuclear radiation? I think that at least pregnant women and children must be evacuated at once from these areas.

I'd like to ask something of all the readers. As religious professionals, should we tolerate the existence of "nuclear powered electricity" that is this dangerous? From various types of faith standpoints, how can we take hold of this present situation? Please let me hear your voice.

Taking Responsibility for Looking Away: The Increasing Anxiety over the Rokkashomura Atomic Fuel Facilities

Rev. Jogaku Fukuzawa

*R*ev. Jogaku Fukuzawa is a priest of the Soto Zen denomination and a member of the Inter Faith Forum for the Review of National Nuclear Policy. Born in 1955 in Aomori Prefecture in northern Japan, he has worked for decades out of a sense of crisis with the basic operation of nuclear fuel cycle facilities in his region. His project, "The Flower and Herb Village", advocates "the building of villages that do not request nuclear fuel" and holds an annual spring tulip festival in Rokkashomura, where these nuclear fuel cycle facilities are located. He is presently in his second year of growing rice based on natural farming methods.

I live in Misawa City in Aomori Prefecture in northern Japan, where there are:

- a center for underground low level nuclear waste disposal
- a factory for enriching uranium
- a temporary storage facility for high level nuclear waste that contains a storage pool of used nuclear fuel
- a reprocessing factory whose final clearance to start operation has been postponed some twenty times or more
- further facilities for the study of an International Thermonuclear Ex perimental Reactor (ITER) that is part of the attempt to build a nuclear fusion reactor
- a Mixed Oxide (MOX) nuclear fuel processing factory

These are all concentrated in this area of facilities curiously developed for "prosperity" in Rokkashomura. From where I am, it is 30 kilometers on a direct line. Almost everyday, I am reminded of the dangers of the Rokkashomura nuclear fuel facility and the nuclear facilities all over the country. We, who have opposed these facilities, have been labeled by the mass media as the anti-atomic fuel and anti-nuclear factions. Among our friends, who tend to be seen as different and separate from regular folks, there are a number who have come down with depression that has been further affected since the Fukushima nuclear incident.

Underestimating of the Crisis

When I think of the phrases, "protecting children from the radiation" and "radiation and life cannot co-exist", I know that a horror that evokes the feeling of "another Chernobyl" has become the reality of this worst-case scenario. And we continue to be flooded with these images again and again everyday by the media. The incident at the Fukushima #1 nuclear facility has brought to light just one fragment of the truth about our national "prosperity". Both our past and present are now being revealed.

Our nuclear energy policy is the work of the so called "atomic village", a self-seeking group of bureaucrats from the Japanese Ministry of Economy, Trade, and Industry (METI) and the Ministry of Education, Culture, Sports, Science, and Technology (MEXT), politicians, electric companies, scholars, and journalists all rolled into one.For this reason, the many people introduced by the media as so-called "nuclear energy experts" only ever say that, "It is safe".

The idea that nuclear energy is "the dream energy that opens the way to a bright future of clean and safe energy" is a preposterous and hollow cover up that is the work of information distortion supported by the giant money of nuclear power.The mass media, which has been tamed by the electric power companies through major sponsorship, does not offer the information that the people really want to know. The Japanese government, which must protect the living situation of its people in facing a crisis within the larger crisis of the tsunami, has underestimated the evolution of the situation, concealed information, repeatedly given empty reports, and not taken practical measures to face the situation even now some four months since the start of the crisis. The government has not properly functioned.

Every time I hear the name of the Nuclear Safety Commission, I am reminded of a scene from the famous documentary made some years back called *Rokkashomura Rhapsody,* directed by Hitomi Kamanaka. In the scene, a question is posed about the still undetermined final disposal of high-level nuclear waste (now vitrified into glass form), and the answer that comes is, "It's ultimately about money of course." It is then revealed that a local authority accepted a huge amount of money. This turned out to be none other than Haruki Madarame, who was a member of the Nuclear Safety Commission. This was a symbolic expression of the destructive arrogance of this country's top organizations, the head of the Nuclear Safety Commission, scientists, and nuclear energy experts.

The Conquest of the Worship of Money

This situation is somewhat like that of the time of the Buddha in India when the worship of fire was popular. It is as if no one has noticed how our country has become caught up in the worship of money.

There is a daily attitude of leaving it up to others. There is also our personal lack of responsibility, concern, and understanding in which we pretend not to see, while saying things like, "I'm busy", "Our lifestyle depends on it", "I don't have time for that", and "I have nothing to do with it". All the while, bureaucrats, electric companies, and politicians are allowed to continue in their arrogant ways. The unmistaken result has been the present Fukushima nuclear disaster and our struggle to overcome it.

In Japan, we harbor 54 nuclear reactors as well as the excessive Rokkashomura nuclear fuel cycle facilities. In this way, there continues today unnoticed, potential situations that go beyond Fukushima. Right now, from the nuclear reactors all over Japan, 235,942 barrels of low level radioactive waste, 13,172 barrels (3,258 tons) of spent nuclear fuel, and 1,338 barrels of high level solid vitrified nuclear waste (a high density radioactive liquid packed into mixed glass and stainless steel containers) have been moved to Rokkashomura.

The past ... the time that is already gone cannot be recovered. The future... the time that has yet to come is a blank slate. Therefore, it all depends on the awareness and choices of each living person. It is not a choice to leave it up to others and not take responsibility, not show concern, and not develop understanding. What will we choose to do now?

I have heard that the traditional Japanese foods of miso soup, pickled vegetables, pickled plums, and brown rice are able to raise the body's immunity against radiation. After the incident, a friend of mine living in Fukushima quickly evacuated the prefecture. Eventually, as his old mother never left, he became resigned to the situation and notified his friends that he was returning to care for his mother. While feeling confused and shaken, I went ahead to send to him last year's pickled plums and to begin to prepare the pickling agent for this year's plums.

Entire series translated by Jonathan Watts with special thanks to Nobuhito Kudo, Editor-in-Chief of the Bukkyo Times, for his support.

Which Way to Peace?
The Role of Japanese Buddhism in Anti-Nuclear Civil Protest

Jonathan Watts

Septmber 11th, 2011: the six-month anniversary of Japan's "triple disaster" and the ten-year anniversary of the "terror attacks" on the United States—the karmic connection or "inter-being" of the events seems clear. The largest anti-nuclear rally in Japan of 60,000 in downtown Tokyo is starting to march after an hour of speeches by some of Japan's leading cultural figures, like Nobel Prize winning novelist Kenzaburo Oe. I have been standing with a lone Buddhist priest carrying a flag proclaiming that followers of the *nenbutsu* (the mantra of Pure Land Buddhists' devotion to Amitabha Buddha) are against nuclear power and militarism. His name is Rev. Hidehito Okochi, a Jodo Pure Land denomination priest and long time environmental-political-social activist. His group, the Inter Faith Forum for the Review of National Nuclear Policy, has been helping families from Fukushima to evacuate the nuclear radiation and find temporary shelter in temples and churches. Next to me is also Nobuhito Kudo, chief editor of the non-sectarian *Bukkyo (Buddhist) Times*, which ran over the summer a series of editorials by anti-nuclear Buddhist activists that included Rev. Okochi. We wonder aloud why amidst this vast array of citizens groups—from labor unions to political parties to small non-profits on every kind of issue—there are no self-identified Buddhist groups ... except for one, the Nipponzan Myohoji.

Nipponzan Myohoji is a tiny denomination of itinerant Japanese Buddhist monks and laypeople devoted to the teachings of the *Lotus Sutra* as presented by Nichiren (1222-82) and the recitation of its mantra called the *daimoku* ("namu-myoho-renge-kyo"). What differentiates them from many similar such groups in Japan is the expression of this faith through continual civil protest for peace, non-violence, and social justice. As I march with them, they chant the *daimoku* in rhythmic tandem with the deafening sounds of handheld drums.

Soon, we come upon a mass of young people who have already begun their own form of street party protest. Dressed in all sorts of costumes befitting Japan's unique *otaku* culture, they bang drums, play instruments, and dance while leading boisterous chants of "We don't need nuclear energy! Let's end it soon!" No, these youth are not the next generation of Japanese political or business leaders. As with the Buddhist groups, I again ponder the conspicuous absence of Japanese university student groups.

The combined energy of chanting-drumming monks and the dancing-drumming youth create a real liveliness and even a sense of connection amongst us. What an unusual thing to do in urban Japan; rub flesh with fellow citizens over shared concerns for society. In a culture where materialism and consumerism have come to dominate the minds of many who at the same time suffer from lost community, alienation, and suicide, this feeling of connecting with strangers over something of actual importance and relevance to our lives gives me a sense of hope for the future here.

The Popular Politicization of Nuclear Energy

While the people of northeast Japan struggled just to secure shelter and basic needs in the aftermath of the massive earthquake and tsunami of March 11, another crisis was unfolding at the Fukushima #1 nuclear reactors that has brought to a head a social crisis building for over a decade. While this crisis is manifold—economic, environmental, social, psychological, and even spiritual—the political crisis over the past year has been perhaps foremost. There has been the inability of the Japanese government to respond to the critical needs of the people in Tohoku, principally in the areas most directly affected by high levels of radiation. There have also been the nationwide political battles over nuclear power and energy policy, symbolized in the fall of the Naoto Kan administration.

This political crisis has not just been one with the nation's central leadership, ongoing since the fall of the Liberal Democratic Party in 2007, the revolving door of prime ministers (six in the last six years), and the continuing uncertainty of the balance of power between elected politicians and entrenched bureaucrats. This crisis has had very strong ramifications on local politics and the sphere of urban civil society. The former issue revolves around the very difficult choice rural communities must make regarding their economic reliance on hosting massive nuclear facilities and the obvious dangers these facilities bring their citizens. The latter issue revolves around how urban citizens—the vast majority of the Japanese population who benefit from the electricity provided by the remotely located nuclear plants—must face the corrupt manner that politicians, bureaucrats, and energy company executives have managed Japanese energy policy, specifically nuclear energy.

Former Prime Minister Naoto Kan attempted to politicize the nuclear issue as much as possible and make it the basis for a popular election on the mandate of his administration. While local elections in rural areas in this period have become battlegrounds for the nuclear issue, there have not been significant national elections yet to serve as a wider popular mandate on the future of Japan's energy policy. Public opinion appears to be in favor of the elimination, either quickly or gradually, of nuclear power, and nuclear activists are seeking to make it an issue for national elections as Italy did in June, striking down plans to build new reactors. In a poll from September 21 conducted by the *Mainichi Shimbun* newspaper, almost two-thirds of respondents indicated they wanted a vote on whether the country should continue to rely so heavily on nuclear power.[1] Outside of such elections, what other mechanisms do Japanese citizens have to confront this crisis, which serves as a linchpin for deciding on the greater overall direction of the nation suffering from economic and social decline for the past decade?

Popular protest would seem to be one very viable option to the Japanese. 2011 was the year of the Arab Spring in the Middle East with popular street protests and people's movements toppling years of entrenched dictatorship. Yet after the years of very active and sometimes

[1] Birmingham, Lucy. "Can Japan's Anti-Nuclear Protesters Keep Its Reactors Shut Down?" *Time Magazine* September 28, 2011

violent labor and student unrest in the 1960s, Japan's citizens have settled into a period of political apathy. This is especially true amongst the youth who have low voter turnout rates[2] and do not share an interest for popular civil protest with their brethren in other parts of the world—such as in the people's political reform movements in other parts of Asia and the Middle East and the anti-globalization street movement culture in the U.S. and Europe. Keio University professor Yoshiaki Kobayashi has said his studies indicate people in their teens and 20s doubt their involvement in society will change it for the better.[3] Indeed, during a June 11 anti-nuclear protest in Tokyo, a young 21-year-old shopper and passerby said, "What can they really do? It looks fun, but if you think anything will change, it's naive."[4]

Meanwhile, spurred on by the unfolding nuclear disaster in Fukushima, 100,000 Germans took to the streets on March 14th to express their concerns over nuclear energy and the energy policy of their country. This was followed by another massive round of nuclear protests all over the country numbering around 200,000 people on March 27, which precipitated Germany's plan to abandon all nuclear power by 2022. While Japan was certainly preoccupied with simply dealing with the extreme emergency of the tsunami and the unfolding nuclear disaster, one of the first nuclear demonstrations held on March 20 in the downtown Tokyo center of Shibuya drew only 1,500 people.

In terms of Japan, however, a significant moment did occur three weeks later on April 10th in a nearby area of Tokyo called Koenji. It started as another small demonstration but through internet social networking—the motor for so many popular protests around the world today—it caught the imagination of thousands of young people, and the numbers eventually swelled to a startling 17,000 people who created a kind of street festival cum protest. One of the organizers of the rally, Hajime Matsumoto, was quoted as saying, "It's epoch-making that so many people gathered without being mobilized by a large organization. It's become powerful

---

[2] Turnout among people under 30 was 66.7% in the 1967 election. It fell below 50% in the 1993 House of Representatives election and has hovered at around 30% to 40% since then. Turnout among those in their 60s has essentially stayed at around 70% to 80% over the past three decades. "Groups hope to halt young voters' apathy: System, rules, fixed candidates all blamed for demographic gap." *Kyodo News*, June 20, 2009.
[3] Ibid.
[4] Tabuchi, Hiroko. "Protests Challenge Japan's Use of Nuclear Power" *New York Times*. June 11, 2011.
[5] "17,500 Rally Against Nuke Plants". *Kyodo News*. April 10, 2011.

because we joined hands over the Internet."[5]

From this point, the anti-nuclear rallies and movement began to grow with regular protest marches in front of the headquarters of the Tokyo Electrical Power Company (TEPCO), owner of the Fukushima reactors. On June 11, the three-month anniversary of the tsunami, there was a nationwide Anti-Nuclear One Million Person Action of demonstrations and other anti-nuclear events held at about 140 sites across Japan, including Tokyo, Osaka, Hiroshima, and also Fukui Prefecture, where a slew of nuclear power plants are located. The largest of these was a rally of 20,000 people in another major hub of Tokyo called Shinjuku. On the sixth month anniversary of the disaster, these numbers swelled even further to the largest rally against nuclear power to date of 60,000 people at Meiji Park in Tokyo. While the movement appears to be continuing to grow, it is ironic that these numbers still do not come close to the number of Germans who took to the streets in the initial days after March 11th.

Nuclear Power, Buddhism, and the Nipponzan Myohoji

What is Buddhism's attitude towards nuclear energy? Buddhism has no central authority to offer a policy, nor does its ethical system—which stays away from absolute commandments while emphasizing the intentional mind of the actor—offer a clear-cut answer. Perhaps the clearest standpoint is that Buddhism's entire ethical system is based on its first precept: to do no harm, or in positive terms, to help sustain life. In this way, nuclear energy with its potential for highly dangerous accidents, the high toxicity of its waste, and the potential to do harm for years into the future would appear to go against Buddhist ethical norms. Joanna Macy, a Buddhist anti-nuclear activist leader since the 1970s in the United States, has stated in her Nuclear Guardianship Ethic, first developed in 1990, that:

Each generation shall endeavor to preserve the foundations of life and well-being for those who come after. To produce and abandon substances that damage following generations is morally unacceptable. Given the extreme toxicity and longevity of radioactive materials, their production must cease. The development of safe, renewable energy sources and non-violent means of conflict resolution is essential to the health and survival of life on Earth. Radioactive materials are not to be regarded as an economic or military resource. [6]

Japanese Buddhist anti-nuclear activists have echoed this sentiment over the past year frequently speaking of the incompatibility of life and nuclear energy.

However, nuclear energy is a particularly personal and sensitive issue for Japanese Buddhists.As victims of the first nuclear bombings at the end of World War II, Japanese Buddhists developed a strong position against nuclear weapons, exemplified by the work of not only Nipponzan Myohoji but also the new lay Buddhist denominations of Soka Gakkai and Rissho Koseikai. However, it appears that nuclear *energy* is considered a different issue for Japanese Buddhists. Since Japan has never possessed nuclear weapons, activism to ban them has allowed Japanese Buddhists to focus over the years more on the larger, global political issues between the United States and the former Soviet Union.

Anti-nuclear energy activism, however, has required a more critical stance towards the existence of nuclear energy development within Japan and its use as a foundation for industrial growth. Such activism veers into a web of much more complicated issues involving criticism of the government, big business, and national development policies—a place that only a few Buddhists will go, like Rev. Tetsuen Nakajima, along with Rev. Okochi, one of the founders of the Inter Faith Forum for the Review of National Nuclear Policy. In an editiorial published on the front page of the *Bukkyo Times* in June, Rev. Nakajima wrote:

The Inter Faith Forum for the Review of National Nuclear Policy in Japan has investigated the history of nuclear development and developed an argument concerning the process of modernization. Japan's modernization began with the shock of Commodore Perry's "black ships" from the United States in

---

[6] http://www.joannamacy.net/nuclearguardianship/nuclear-guardianship-ethic.html

1854. Japan then proceeded to develop national slogans such as, "Quit Asia, Enter Europe", "Cultural Progress", "Rich Nation, Strong Military", and then sacrificed many precious lives in World War II. However, after the war, we continued on this path. I have spoken of the new tacit slogans "Quit Asia, Enter America", "Faith in Scientific Technique", and "Great Economic Nation". Large-scale production, large-scale consumption, and large-scale disposal, as personified in the giant nuclear power crowd, became an extension of the modernization process since the coming of the black ships. At all times, there has been the demand for quantification, speed and pleasure, and economism. This kind of awareness has supported "The Myth of Need" [for nuclear energy] at its roots. Now, we have to undergo a deep process of self-reflection.[7]

Developing a critical position towards central political and economic power is not something that institutionalized religion anywhere in the world is apt to engage in. It is even more so in terms of Japanese Buddhism. Since the end of its 250-year patronage under the feudal Tokugawa government and a period of persecution by the new Shinto oriented Meiji government in the mid 1800s, Japanese Buddhism has been in a continual cycle of accommodation towards political power and social opinion. In the seventy years leading up to World War II, Japanese Buddhism developed itself in accord with nationalist development agendas and ultimately became a pro-active supporter of the war effort.[8]

Since the end of the war and the deep disillusionment of Japanese with religion and politics, a strong secular social ethic has created a deeper threat to Japanese Buddhism. This position of weakness in the

[7] Nakajima, Tetsuen. "Religious Activities which also Issuing Warnings: The 3 Structures of Discrimination: Rural Regions, Nuclear Contaminated Work, Children" *Bukkyo (Buddhist) Times* June 2, 2011 (translation by author)

[8] Watts, Jonathan & Okano, Masazumi. "Reconstructing Priestly Identity and Roles and the Development of Socially Engaged Buddhism in Contemporary Japan" in *The Handbook of Contemporary Japanese Religions* (Leiden, Netherlands: E.J. Brill, 2012)

public sphere has meant that Buddhist denominations have not felt the courage or strength to speak out on important social issues, much less criticize national development agendas like nuclear energy.[9] The newer Buddhist denominations, like Soka Gakkai and Rissho Koseikai, grew rapidly after the war due to their more modern appeal. However, their growth into massive organizations made them a target for electoral power, and they have to a certain extent become politicized while losing their independent moral voice to speak on political and economic issues.

Nipponzan Myohoji serves as one exception to this above pattern. It has been called, "unusual, perhaps even unique among Japanese Buddhist groups, for its commitment to civil protest."[10] It is their size, as a tiny fringe denomination, that allows them to be politically radical; or rather, perhaps, it is their teachings that have prevented them from becoming a mass organization in the first place. Like other Japanese Buddhist groups, they have an ambiguous history in terms of Japanese imperialism before and during World War II. Their founder, Rev. Nichidatsu Fujii (1885-1985), initially ventured into Manchuria and China and then onwards to other parts of Asia as a missionary and chaplain to Japanese troops. A brief encounter with Mahatma Gandhi in 1933 and his experience of the Indian independence movement helped to clarify his views on Buddhism and social change:

> The people [of India] were trying to reform the government without resorting to violence. If they succeeded in their attempt, theirs would be the ideal form of government. For this reason, I was very interested in what was happening in India ... Nevertheless Japan ... was indifferent to the Indian independence movement. Not only did she not cooperate with the movement, she even sided with the British

---

[9] Rev. Hiroaki Osada, a Pure Land Jodo Shin Otani priest and member of the Inter Faith Forum for the Review of National Nuclear Policy, has made the connection with pre-War unquestioning acceptance of the Emperor with such acceptance post-War of the nation's nuclear energy policy. Isa, Kyoko. "Anti-Nukes" Remains Fixed on Life: Declarations from the Religious World Come One after Another." *Asahi Shimbun*. December 12, 2011 (translated by author).

[10] Stone, Jacqueline I. "Nichiren's Activist Heirs: Sōka Gakkai, Risshō Kōseikai, Nipponzan Myōhōji." In *Action Dharma: New Studies in Engaged Buddhism*, edited by Christopher Queen, Charles Prebish, and Damien Keown, 63-94. (London: RoutledgeCurzon, 2003), p.78.

rulers ... I keenly felt that it was not good for Japan, with its proximity to India and her traditional ties through Buddhism, to refrain from helping Indians achieve independence or to suppress their movement. I could not straight-forwardly tell the Japanese Government and people, and even if I could, they would not listen. So I decided to cooperate with the independence movement led by Gandhi and pray for its success. [11]

Out of the tradition of Hinduism, there emerged Buddhism which embodies the idea of non-violence in its most complete form. It was indeed an important development. Buddhism is not only necessary for promoting a peaceful revolution in today's India but also is a tool of spiritual guidance with which to save all the human race who are involved in acts of violence and wars; it encourages abolition of all means of violence ... My wish for the eternity of the Buddha *(genrai kike)* and the non-violent revolution which Gandhi advocated came from the same origin, the doctrine of Buddhism ... This concept cannot be fully expressed in the term "revolution", and in Buddhism it is referred to as "attainment of Buddhahood". The ultimate revolutionary aim of Buddhism consists in having both man and the world attain Buddhahood. Completely detached from things like political power, the human race should leap above all such conflicts. This is the true essence of Buddhist revolution. [12]

Despite these words above, it appears Fujii had not yet fully embraced non-violence as evidenced in Myohoji monks acting as chaplains to the Japanese army [13] and presenting top military leaders with Buddha relics in the early days of the war.[14] The experience of the devastation at the end of the war, especially with the bombings of Hiroshima and Nagasaki, finally pushed Fujii to his decisive stance.

---

[11] Fujii, Nichidatsu. *My Non-Violence: An Autobiography of a Japanese Buddhist* Trans. T. Yamaori. (Tokyo: Japan Buddha Sangha Press, 1975), p.67-68.

[12] Fujii. *My Non-Violence*, p.80-81.

[13] Robert Kisala. *Prophets of Peace: Pacifism and Cultural Identity in Japan's New Religions.* (Honolulu: University of Hawaii Press, 1999) p. 51

[14] Fujii. *My Non-Violence*, p. 87-88.

What led me to assert non-resistance, disarmament, and the abolition of war was not my encounter with Mr. Gandhi. When the atom bombs were dropped on Hiroshima and Nagasaki, and I saw hundreds of thousands of innocent women and children die as though burned at the stake and poisoned, victims of a tragedy unprecedented in human history; when I saw Japan forced to accept unconditional surrender, then I understood the madness, folly, and barbarousness of modern war. [15]

In the post-war period, many other Japanese Buddhist groups shifted remarkably quickly to positions advocating world peace, the abolishing of nuclear weapons, and the closing of American military bases in Japan. A number of writers, including D.T. Suzuki, have questioned the sincerity of these sudden shifts. It took until 1987 for the first major Japanese denomination to issue a public apology over their active support of the war.[16] However, one still must be impressed by especially Myohoji and the other new Buddhist denominations for shifting from a stance of tacit support for violent nationalism[17] to one of a non-violent internationalism based largely in an ecumenical interpretation of Buddhism.

Yet what is it that separates Myohoji from other Buddhist groups in their unique activism of civil protest? Perhaps the answer lies Fujii's ascetic, missionary ethic. While sharing a missionary ethic with the many other *Lotus Sutra* based new Buddhist denominations, Myohoji is unique among them for being centered around monastics and not householder, lay leaders who have tended to espouse conservative, middle class social values. Further, unlike the majority of traditional Japanese Buddhist priests who have come to marry, have families, and engage in lay lifestyles since the Meiji Period social reforms, Fujii and

---

[15] Stone, Jacqueline I. "Nichiren's Activist Heirs: Sōka Gakkai, Risshō Kōseikai, Nipponzan Myōhōji.", p.79.

[16] Five denominations have made any such substantive declarations: both the Higashi (1987) and Nishi (1992) branches of the Jodo Shin denomination, the Soto Zen (1992) denomination, and the Myoshinji and Tenryuji branches of the Rinzai Zen denomination (2001) (Victoria, Brian. 2006. *Zen at War*. Lanham, MD: Rowman & Littlefield Publishers) as well as the Jodo denomination in 2008.

[17] Myohoji, Rissho Koseikai, and Soka Gakkai all come out of the Nichiren tradition, some of whose leaders developed particularly virulent forms of militaristic nationalism in the Meiji Period under the banner of Nichiren-ism, Stone. Jacqueline I. "Nichiren's Activist Heirs: Sōka Gakkai, Risshō Kōseikai, Nipponzan Myōhōji." 83-84.

his disciples have maintained unmarried monastic lifestyles supported by the donations of followers and not the income gained by doing funerals and memorial services. Yet unlike traditional monastics who remain cloistered in famous temples like Eihei-ji or on holy mountains like Mt. Hiei or Mt. Koya, Fujii was a missionary dedicated to encountering people in the world to spread the "good news" of the *Lotus Sutra* in the way the Buddha walked through India. His endurance of austerities to spread the teachings in the cold of Manchuria from 1917-23 created a culture in Myohoji of ascetic sacrifice for religious goals, which later expressed themselves as socio-political goals for peace and social justice.

Nipponzan Myohoji has developed a complete dedication to fulfilling the larger aims of the *Lotus Sutra* through civil protest, specifically on issues surrounding militarism such as U.S. military bases in Japan and nuclear weapons. Myohoji first began to participate in civil protest during the anti-nuclear movement touched off by the exposure of Japanese fishermen to American nuclear testing on Bikini Atoll in 1954.[18] They also began participating in protests against American military bases in Japan—one of the most memorable being their solidarity with farmers and local citizens in facing police brutality at sit-ins opposing the Sunagawa Airforce Base in 1957.[19]

Myohoji has complemented this domestic activism with international activism: joining anti-nuclear protests in the United States in the 1980s, leading a peace walk through Central and North America in 1992 to commemorate the 500th anniversary of Columbus' arrival in the New World and the subsequent oppression of indigenous peoples; leading another peace walk from Auschwitz to Hiroshima in 1995 on the 50th anniversary of the end of World War II; participating in numerous peace walks with Maha Ghosananda in Cambodia in the 1990s; and attempting to be a peace witness during the civil war in Sri Lanka that led to the murder of one of its monks in 1984. While having long participated in marches against nuclear arms, on April 24, 2010, they participated in a march to protest nuclear energy and its perception as an alternative green energy to CO_2 generating fossil fuels in Limerik, Pennsylvania

---

[18] Stone, Jacqueline I. "Nichiren's Activist Heirs: Sōka Gakkai, Risshō Kōseikai, Nipponzan Myōhōji." p. 77.

[19] Fujii. *My Non-Violence,* p. 118.

(USA) at the site of the Exelon's Limerick Nuclear Generating Station.

In the wake of the unfolding nuclear crisis at the Fukushima #1 facility, Nipponzan Myohoji was the first Japanese Buddhist denomination to issue a declaration against nuclear power on March 20 stating in part:

> We must understand how "the use of nuclear power" and "the sustainability of life" are incompatible … We cannot allow Japan to become a country that spreads radioactivity. In order to take a step in showing our self-critical reflection and revival, we must show to the world first that we can stop the Hamaoka Nuclear Power Plant.

One of the first successes of this new anti-nuclear movement was then Prime Minister Naoto Kan's unilateral decision on May 6th to close the Hamaoka Plant, an outdated complex located on the Pacific Ocean on a major geological fault line only 200 kms from Tokyo.

On the other hand, it took over six months for any of the traditional Buddhist denominations to issue such statements. The Japan Buddhist Federation, which serves as the representative organization of all the traditional Buddhist denominations of Japan, issued a statement on December 1st, almost nine months after the disaster began, saying, "We will strive to reduce our dependence on such nuclear power that threatens life and to realize a society based on sustainable energy."

As we reach the one-year anniversary of the disaster, Rissho Koseikai and Soka Gakkai, leaders of the anti-nuclear arms movement in the Japanese Buddhist world, have remained stunningly silent on the issue thus far. While both groups have integrated renewable energy positions and some basic initiatives into their activities, they have made no public declarations on nuclear energy even as the notoriously conservative traditional Buddhist world has started to move forward on the issue. Unofficial sources have said that the high number of followers in these denominations who work in management positions in the nuclear facilities in rural areas make it a difficult issue for them to speak out against openly.

Yet Rev. Takao Takeda, head of Myohoji's main temple in Tokyo, points out that following the Pope's own critical comments on nuclear energy in June[20], Japanese Catholics have made critical statements on Japan's nuclear energy policy while also having members in senior positions in the nuclear energy business. On November 8th, the Japan Catholic Pontifical Council released a statement calling on the immediate discontinuation of all nuclear power within Japan.[21] Even a large number of local government officials and members of RENGO—the 6.8-million member federation of labor unions which normally never goes against nuclear power because many members are nuclear industry employees—participated in the September 11 rally at Meiji Park.[22] Further, there are numerous traditional Buddhist priests, like Rev. Nakajima, who live in communities sustained by nuclear power plants yet have engaged in activism against them for many years. The disconnect between Rissho Koseikai and Soka Gakkai's forthrightness on nuclear arms and silence on nuclear energy is puzzling and naturally raises questions about the sincerity of their previous work.[23]

Myohoji, on the other hand, has always taken a critical position on insider corruption between Japanese business and government and Japan's continued alliance with the United States and its political and economic policies. With the experience of the atomic bombings,

---

[20] http://www.catholicnewsagency.com/news/pope-benedict-calls-for-clean-energy/

[21] Isa, Kyoko. "Anti-Nukes" Remains Fixed on Life: Declarations from the Religious World Come One after Another." *Asahi Shimbun,* December 12, 2011 (translated by author).

[22] Birmingham, "Can Japan's Anti-Nuclear Protesters Keep Its Reactors Shut Down?" *Time Magazine,* September 28, 2011.

[23] As this volume was going to press, Daisaku Ikeda, the President of Soka Gakkai International, issued the most far reaching comments by the head of a Japanese Buddhist denomination on the nuclear energy issue in his annual January 26 peace proposal, stating: "I therefore urge a rapid transition to an energy policy that is not reliant on nuclear power. Japan should collaborate with other countries that are at the forefront of efforts to introduce renewable energy sources and undertake joint development projects to achieve substantial cost reductions in these technologies. Japan should also take on, as its mission, efforts to promote the kind of technological innovation that will facilitate the introduction of new energy sources in developing countries that currently struggle with this issue. In effecting this transition, it is necessary that adequate measures be taken to foster alternative industrial bases in communities that have been economically dependent on nuclear power generating facilities and have contributed to the national power supply. ... In point of fact, the damage to both human health and the natural environment from exposure to radioactivity is exactly the same for an equivalent dose whatever the source—the actual use of nuclear weapons, the release of radioactivity accompanying the development, production and testing of these weapons, or an accident at a nuclear power plant." Ikeda, Daisaku. "Human Security and Sustainability: Sharing Reverence for the Dignity of Life (2012 Peace Proposal)". January, 26, 2012, p.14. http://www.sgi.org/assets/pdf/peaceproposal2012.pdf.

Fujii developed a philosophy espousing the power of Buddhism as a civilizational force for peace and non-violence over the scientific materialism of the West, and especially the United States, that would only lead to war and the destruction of the environment.[24] While Fujii was also critical of the violent means used in socialist and communist movements [25] , his views on technology and colonialism naturally led Myohoji to an anti-capitalist and anti-American stance that connected to the Japanese labor and student movements of the 1950s and 60s.

However, their insistence on non-violence and the power of religious civilization also made them attractive for certain radical youth who identified with the student movement but saw a missing spiritual component to it. Ultimately, Myohoji's leftist political ideology and long association itself with the Communist Party of Japan has surely kept it as a marginal group within Japan over the years, even as it has grown to some level of fame internationally for its overseas activism. Overall, this image of confrontational, social activism and its political associations have been an important reason why the average Japanese has avoided participating in the recent anti-nuclear protests. Indeed, Rev. Takeda estimates that out of the 60,000 people taking part in the demonstration at Meiji Park on September 11, at least 20,000 of them were connected with the Communist Party.

Youth Division

It is in part the legacy of the violent and confrontational past of the socialist and student movements of the 1960s in Japan that has kept many university students away from these protests. In the 1960s, ironically, it was the students at elite schools like Tokyo University and Waseda University who led some of the strongest left-wing movements that would take over campuses for months.[26] Yet, in a discussion session with the aforementioned Rev. Hidehito Okochi and a group of students from the elite Keio University in Tokyo in May, some students remarked

---

[24] Kisala, *Prophets of Peace*, p. 161.

[25] "What is wrong about Marxism is that it allowed one to adopt violence and take the lives of others in the pursuit of his rights. Murder, whether committed by a Capitalist nation or a Communist nation, is the same." Fujii, Nichidatsu. *Buddhism for World Peace*. Translated by Yumiko Miyazaki. Tokyo: Japan-Bharat Sarvodaya Mitra Sangha, 1980. p. 21.

[26] Leong, Adriene. "Japanese Youth Too Disillusioned to Vote". Foreign Correspondence Club of Japan Scholarship Ward. April 2008. http://www.fccj.or.jp/node/3374.

that it was not in keeping with Japanese culture to express one's views in such a confrontational manner and that participating in candlelight vigils would be more appropriate.

Rev. Okochi, himself an alumnus of Keio who participated in the student movement as a youth, remarked that perhaps it is not so much that young Japanese are politicallyapathetic but rather politically ignorant. He remarks that in today's Japan, the young are too self absorbed with their own lives, and political issues are not something they are taught to be involved in or care about. Rev. Takeda of Myohoji echoes this sentiment, feeling that the responsibility very much lies with the generation of parents who have raised their children to be politically disconnected.

This apathy among university students is in contrast to the youth jamboree portrayed at the beginning of this chapter. There indeed seems to be a split, which reflects the well documented growth in class divisions in Japan—a country that prided itself on being predominantly "middle class" throughout the post war period of economic growth. The youth who are university students, especially those at elite schools, are still invested in the social model that has served Japan since the end of the war: study hard, work hard, enter a good company, build a family, and contribute to the building of the nation. However, the bursting of the economic bubble in the early 1990s and the advent of liberalization and structural re-adjustment under the Koizumi regime in the 2000s swept away most of the benevolent features of Japanese capitalism, such as life time employment. Even for university graduates, especially at lower level schools, finding a well-paying, rewarding corporate job is not easy. Regular overtime and temp work is common, and more and more people are slipping through the cracks of an overwhelmed social welfare system.

In this age of suicide—rates in Japan have been over 30,000 since 1998—there is a growing class of young "drop outs" going by various names: *freeta* – for those who prize leisure over career (over 3 million); NEET – for those "not in education, employment or training"; *futoko* – for those who refuse to go to school; and the most extreme, *hikikomori* – for those who refuse to leave their bedrooms or houses, often for years on end (over 2 million).[27] It is especially from these *freeta* and NEET that a group of young Japanese are emerging who are tied with larger global trends in alternative living, organic food, environ-

---

[27] Ibid.

mentalism, and even political activism, much of it spread though social networking, the internet, and even hip hop. The seminal rally at Koenji in early April was one of the first expressions of the political potential of this movement. A May 7th rally that drew 5,000 culminated in the heart of Tokyo's youth culture in Shibuya and ended up as a wild rave party taking over the streets while Rankin' Taxi—a reggae hip hop artist who wrote a popular new song called "You Can't See It, And You Can't Smell It Either"[28] —blasted his anti-nuclear rap from a mobile DJ stand. This is certainly not the culture of well-dressed and well-mannered elite Japanese university students, yet it is also not the culture of the violent student confrontations of the 1960s. Political activism has evolved since then, and while these young Japanese dropouts are angry about many things in their society, they are embracing something positive in the post-modern global environmental and alternative culture movements.

Which Way to Peace? Social Welfare and Social Justice

There is a particular tension in the way religious groups, in this case Buddhist groups, approach social engagement. The two poles of this tension can be understood as social welfare activities and social justice activities. The former focuses on work that aids and supports those in need in society and takes a conservative stance towards existing and established power structures. The latter focuses on work that changes or transforms existing power structures to root out the causes that make people needy and disadvantaged in society.

From the extreme end of the social welfare pole, the most conservative Buddhist groups in Japan—from the traditional sects to a number of the larger new denominations—have established a variety of social welfare activities, such as providing kindergartens and day care centers, establishing schools and universities, and supporting the elderly. Many of these groups have extended such domestic activities into the international sphere, providing significant funding and establishing projects for social welfare in poor countries in Asia and Africa. Their conservative stance towards power structures most often expresses itself in disengagement on difficult political issues and avoidance in taking strong moral positions in public; for example, the issue of the change

---

[28] Grunebaum, Dan. "Japan's New Wave of Protest Songs". New York Times, June 30, 2011

of Article 9 in the Japanese constitution to develop a proper military or the corrupt ties between the government and electric companies on the development of nuclear power.

Many Buddhist groups have attempted to temper this domestic conservativism with a kind of internationalism largely focused on activities for "world peace". Both the traditional and new Buddhist denominations, including the most social justice oriented Nipponzan Myohoji, have engaged in ongoing prayer activities for world peace. These tend to be the most conservative and "safe" forms of expressing political sentiments for peace through the greater religious aspiration for peace. Others groups, most notably Soka Gakkai and Rissho Koseikai, have devoted energy to more socially engaged forms of peace work by developing campaigns against nuclear arms and creating conferences and even entire organizations, such as the World Conference on Religion and Peace co-founded by Rissho Koseikai.

However, this internationalism has largely masked a continued domestic conservatism on issues of social justice. This is most keenly seen in Soka Gakkai's creation of the Komeito political party, which was over the years a key coalition partner of the Liberal Democratic Party and its 54-year run in power until 2007. While Komeito appears to have tried to temper the LDP's conservativism, it never pulled out of the coalition for attempts to change Article 9 or for its cabinet ministers' visits to the Japanese war memorial at Yasukuni Shrine that also houses Japan's war criminals. In terms of both of these groups, their silence on the nuclear energy issue has been striking.

On the furthest end of this spectrum lie groups who actively work on social justice issues both within and without Japan. The headquarters of traditional Buddhist denominations still lag far behind in engagement on this level. However, their more decentralized power structures have afforded individual priests, as we have seen in this article, to engage in a variety of forms of social engagement. Further, a number of what are called Buddhist NGOs, informally connected to denominational headquarters, have engaged in certain social justice issues on the international level, such as the rights of children, women, and marginalized groups in areas of war and conflict. Still these Buddhist NGOs rarely lead campaigns within Japan to raise public awareness of human rights abuses based on political oppression in places such as Burma. Such activities are again only done by highly motivated individual priests, such as Rev. Okochi, who usually joins separate non-religious NGO groups within Japan working on such issues. Occasionally, these individuals are able to mobilize enough priests to form non-official denominational groups on social justice issues, such as the variety of denominational groupings called Article 9 Groups *(kyujo-no-kai)* to support the preservation of Japan's constitutional ban on a proper military force.

As we have seen, Nipponzan Myohoji is the only denomination that actively engages in the most extreme forms of social justice work in civil protest. Many Japanese keep clear of such civil protest due to the association of such activities with the confrontational and sometimes violent student and socialist movement of the 1960s. This is ironic because Nipponzan Myohoji more than any other Buddhist group espouses a doctrine of strict non-violence. It is in many ways due to Gandhi's influence on their work that they have made a clear distinction between a pacifism that avoids a critique of social, political, and economic structures and a pacifism that engages with these structures yet adheres to the practice of active non-violence.

One of Gandhi's seminal concepts of non-violence is that to not oppose the exploitation and violence towards another is to actually support it. In this way, Myohoji's confrontational yet non-violent engagement in civic protest is perhaps more true to the ethic of peace than the other denominations' prayers and conferences on peace that fail to confront the structural mechanisms supporting Japan's use of nuclear energy and complicity in American military policy in the Middle East and Asia. One wonders that if Nipponzan Myohoji had the resources to express this distinction to more people, a greater number of both Buddhists and common people might discover civil protest and social justice work as an important component of social change. Rev. Takeda in response to the reticence of Buddhists and common Japanese to engage in civil protest says that they can do other things to work on this issue, such as join petition campaigns to change national energy policy and more actively express their opinions in the media.

Outside of Japan, this Buddhist style of active non-violent social change work (also developed by other religions) has been not only articulated but practiced by groups in Sri Lanka, Thailand, Tibet, India, Cambodia, Burma, Vietnam, and the United States. Unfortunately, Japanese Buddhism's internationalism has not developed a deep enough dialogue with these groups to be sufficiently influenced into mobilizing their own denominations in Japan to engage on such a level. As I have outlined above, Japanese Buddhism is certainly socially engaged, yet if it could develop more mature forms of social justice activity then it could develop a much more powerful and comprehensive social engagement.

Explaining the Sin of Nuclear Power: Symposium at Soto Zen's main temple Eihei-ji Spreads the No Nuke Movement amongst the Buddhist World

Aso Izuta & Kei Sato

With the restarting of the Genkai nuclear power plant on November 2nd by the Kyushu Electric Power Company (KEPCO) in Saga Prefecture and the reconfirmation of the export of nuclear power to Vietnam by the Noda Administration, we can see the revival of the nuclear power faction in Japan in one great leap. On the other hand, Eihei-ji, one of the main temples of the Soto Zen denomination with over eight million followers, held a two-day symposium to consider our lifestyles and a way of living from the viewpoint of "de-nuclearization". Could this be the starting point of a great wave?

On the stage, a hanging scroll of the slender figure of Yoryu Kannon drew many gazes. With willow branch in hand, she symbolizes flexibility to bend to the will of all beings as willow branches to the wind. With the offering of incense, the lighting of candles, and the sound of chanting reverberating through the hall, the symposium with the theme, "Caring for Life: The Way to Live without Choosing Nuclear Power" began.

The conference venue was a public facility in Eihei-ji town in Fukui Prefecture that around 200 people crowded into. One could see priests with robes dotted throughout the audience. The speakers were Kenichi Hasegawa, a 58 year-old dairy farmer from Iita-te village in Fukushima—a radiation hot spot located outside of the 30 km exclusion zone from the Fukushima #1 nuclear facility that on December 5th still had a radiation reading of 2.039 microsieverts/hour. The other speaker was Rev. Tetsuen Nakajima, the sixty-nine year-old abbot of Myotsu-ji, a Shingon denomination temple in the nearby area of Obama City and an activist in the anti-nuclear campaign for over 40 years.

Hasegawa addressed the audience first, and while showing photos and video on a screen, explained the situation after the nuclear incident in Fukushima in March, saying, "If you took a measurement near the houses in these areas using a dosimeter, the needle went off the scale exceeding 100 micro-sieverts. The government has muzzled attempts to inform the local inhabitants of these high levels. Experts have continually said the areas are now 'safe', and there have been no efforts to evacuate people."

Hasegawa went on to talk about the heartbreak of putting down his dairy cows, leaving his hometown, and watching his whole life built up over thirty-five years come to an end. A fellow dairy farmer friend in a note left behind after hanging himself wrote, "If only the nuclear incident hadn't happened." A 102 year-old elderly person from the area said before taking his life, "I don't want to be a burden to others in the evacuation". During Hasegawa's talk there could be heard sobs from the audience.

Hasegawa explained further that, "Pigs are eating the corpses of cows who have died of starvation. This is the present situation in Iita-te village". Next month there will be an experiment in decontamination of topsoil in which 400 square meters will cost 600 million yen. Hasegawa has doubts about the government's plan to have people return to the village saying, "It's not just about the radiation that has become stuck on things. Can the radiation that wafts through the air everywhere also be decontaminated? Further, it will be impossible to decontaminate the forests. Even if we do go back, it'll be impossible to resume farming, and it is not an environment for young people to have and raise children."

Rev. Nakajima then addressed the audience pointing out the "sin" of nuclear power that has given birth to more than 470,000 nuclear contaminated workers in the past 40 years. He emphasized that, "Fundamentally, Japan's modernist spirituality does not bother to look at the negative side of the goal of 'Quit Asia, Enter Europe' (a slogan developed by the Japanese government in the 19th century during its initial industrial drive). Japan today is caught up in the ethos of 'public sacrifice for personal service' rather than 'personal sacrifice for public service.' We must begin by changing this society of extravagant and wasteful energy use."

One of the conference participants, a 62 year-old Fukui housewife named Yoko Watanabe, remarked with admiration that, "We have had anti-nuclear gatherings here and there in this community, but I think it's very significant that a Buddhist temple has hosted this one. All of these conversations have energized and impressed me." On the other hand, the Wakasa Bay, where a cluster of nuclear power plants are lined up, is also a region of many Soto Zen followers. Amongst these followers, there are many connected to the nuclear industry here, and so the stance the temple adopts is very complicated. In this way, the title of the symposium also received a number of negative responses from such people.

Rev. Tesshin Matsubara, the Vice Administrator of Eihei-ji and head of the organizing committee for the symposium remarked, "The point is not about approving or disapproving of nuclear power." Rev. Shokoku Nishida, the head of the Department of Propagation, said, "It is not that Eihei-ji is starting an anti-nuclear campaign. The necessary evil that lurks behind the existing system of nuclear power is the lifestyle of unchecked greed. I am proposing that this is what we need to re-examine." As the tension in the hall rose at this point, tape recorders and video recorders were asked to be turned off.

Afterwards, at the press conference held by Eihei-ji, questions arose about the connection with the temple and nuclear power, such as how the Monju Fast Breeder Reactor and the Fugen Advanced Thermal Reactor were named after the two bodhisattvas Monju (Manjusri, the bodhisattva of wisdom) and Fugen (Samantabhadra, the bodhisattva of practice and meditation). According to Eihei-ji, the then Chairman of the Power Reactor and Nuclear Fuel Development Corporation of Japan, Susumu Kiyonari, visited Eihei-ji and explained to a Zen master, "We named [the reactors after Monju and Fugen] to receive the benefits of the bodhisattva's wisdom and compassion." The master is reported to have responded, "That is fine". In response to a reporter's question, "Did the temple declare such approval?", Rev. Matsubara denied so saying, "That cannot be confirmed". He acknowledged that, "Eihei-ji has done nothing concerning nuclear power," and repeated that, "It has been acknowledged that nuclear power is not compatible with the theory of the earth as sentient life."[1]

A 67 year-old Soto priest from Fukuoka City named Rev. Wajo Kansha praised Eihei-ji saying, "It's not just now. Eihei-ji has already been doing good work in this area." For example, after the nuclear disaster in Chernobyl, his wife, Taeko Kansha, wrote the popular book *It's Still Not Too Late* (1987), which had a strong influence on individuals joining the anti-nuclear movement.

A person connected with Eihei-ji said that at present, "Soto-shu as a denomination has no clear intention". However, it is very true that there are concerned priests at Soto's other main temple, Soji-ji in Yokohama City, who want to support this work. Rev. Kansha further remarked that, "From now, I'm not sure if all the Buddhist denominations will exert their influence on this matter. However, not just Soto but all Buddhist denominations should begin the work of rethinking about nuclear power. This is my hope."

Fukui Prefecture: The Number One Spot for the Establishment of Nuclear Power in Japan

In Fukui Prefecture, there are the following facilities run by the Kansai Electric Power Company (KEPCO):
- 3 reactors at the Mihahama facility
- 4 reactors at the Oi facility
- 4 reactors at the Takahama facility

and the following facilities run by the Japan Atomic Power Company:
- 2 reactors with 2 more planned at the Tsuruga facility
which also hosts
- the Monju Fast Breeder Reactor and
- the Fugen Advanced Thermal Reactor which is currently shut down and awaiting decommissioning.

---

[1] *The Bukkyo Times* reported on November 17th about this press conference and the naming of the reactors as follows: "There was a debate among Zen priests over the naming. However, there is no evidence that priests were directly involved in giving the names Monju and Fugen. In an article from *the Bukkyo Times* dated June 6, 1970, there is a written contribution by Susumu Kiyonari that mentions 'Buddhism and nuclear power' and 'the name of Monju and Fugen'. Kiyonari himself had a good awareness of the horror of nuclear power when naming the reactors. He also had a strong interest in Buddhism, which led him to study it. In this account, there is no mention of a 'certification' in the 'naming of (the reactor)' in 1970. This is what is in the published account of the time."

At present the only ones that are active are Mihahama #2, Oi #2, and Takahama #2 and #3. In February of 2012, all of these reactors will be halted for scheduled inspections. On October 28, KEPCO submitted to the Nuclear and Industrial Safety Agency (NISA), which is within the Ministry of Economy Trade and Industry (METI), the first results of the necessary "safety evaluation" in order to restart operation of the Oi #3 reactor that is undergoing scheduled inspection. The submission of safety inspections has begun for all reactors in the country. KEPCO, which has a higher degree of reliance on nuclear power at 40% of capacity, is aiming to restart its reactors by spring 2012. However, the governor of Fukui Province, Kazumi Ishikawa, has established conditions for safety preparations that include lessons from the Fukushima incident and unforeseen situations that could arise with the resumption of operations.

The Japan Buddhist Federation: A Lifestyle without Dependence on Nuclear Power

The Japan Buddhist Federation (JBF) was created by the traditional Buddhist denominations and associations from all regions of Japan. On December 1st, they will hold their meeting of Board of Directors to create a declaration and adopt a course of action concerning the Fukushima nuclear incident.

Rev. Jitetsu Nara, Head of the General Affairs Division, explained that, "In asking each denomination and its followers, we found that their answers differed on how to deal with the nuclear issue. Nowadays, events like the one Eihei-ji hosted are appearing. It is not just large temples but also small ones that are grappling in various ways with the tsunami and nuclear disasters. In this way, we wanted to inquire as to what kind of joint declaration we could make from the entire traditional Buddhist world."

In a statement from JBF on August 25th, President Rev. Kono Taitsu said, "The nuclear reactor incident has become a subject of our thoughts." He appealed, "In order that this type of incident does not happen a second time, we must re-examine and adjust our daily way of living." Rev. Nara notes that in the present declaration there is the idea that, "In parallel with the dialogue with President Taitsu, we wanted to also do something concrete. The phrase 'anti-nuclear' should not be used because of its political connotations. I think we should instead speak of a lifestyle without dependence on nuclear power."

There are about 60 temples within the 30 km exclusion zone of the Fukushima reactors, and it was unavoidable that together with their lay followers these priests and their families had to evacuate. JBF is now supporting each temple to engage in compensation negotiations with TEPCO. In this way, the incident is still unresolved, and as long as the fear of radiation contamination exists, nuclear power will be a major theme in the Buddhist world.

Editorial Comment:

At the risk of speaking in a sinful manner, we feel that since the nuclear incident, the actions of the religious world have been naïve and unsophisticated. The lives of many tens of thousands of people have been destroyed, and the children, filled with fear, cannot speak of their future dreams. In the face of this tragedy, there are certainly many things that religious professionals should be doing. To begin with, we would like them to want to say "No" to nuclear power. Is there a reason to hesitate here?

Translated by Jonathan Watts
from the Tokyo Shimbun
November 3, 2011

The Japan Buddhist Federation Appeal for a Lifestyle without Dependence on Nuclear Power

*T**he Japan Buddhist Federation is the association of 104 traditional, mainstream Buddhist denominations in Japan, representing more than 90 percent of all Buddhist organizations in Japan.*

December 1, 2011

The spread of radioactive contamination due to the meltdown at the Tokyo Electric Power Company's Fukushima #1 Nuclear Power Facility has caused many people to forcibly evacuate their homes and live as refugees. They suffer through their days in anger that they have no place to reside and in anxiety of having no prospects for the future. Many families with infants and small children live with worries of damaged health due to the radiation, feeling threatened about their lives. Further, we cannot deny the possibility of widespread radioactive contamination affecting not only Japan but also the global environment and ecosystem, threatening all kinds of life, not just human.

Japan is the only country in the world that has ever been hit with nuclear weapons. A great amount of human life was lost then, and those who survived the attack continue to suffer radiation sickness even until this day. So that humanity will not make the same mistake again, we Japanese through our tragedy and suffering have continued to show the people of the world the preciousness of life. Based in the spirit of Buddhism, the Japan Buddhist Federation has been working toward the realization of world peace and societies where each and every life is respected.

At the same time, however, we Japanese have also been expanding our desire for more comfortable and convenient lifestyles. In the shadow of the pursuit for convenience, there lies the reality that the nuclear meltdown in Fukushima has caused the people of that area to live everyday in fear for their lives. In this way, we must deeply reflect on how we have allowed this nuclear plant disaster to endanger a peaceful way of living and life itself.

We, the Japan Buddhist Federation, will strive to reduce our dependence on such nuclear power that threatens life and to realize a society based on sustainable energy. We must choose a path in which personal happiness is harmonized with human welfare, instead of wishing for prosperity at the expense of others. Finally, we would like to make an appeal for building societies that protect each and every life through each individual confronting this issue themselves by reflecting on their own lifestyle, letting go of excessive materialistic greed, finding contentment in the feeling of moderation, and doing their best to realize living in humility with nature.

Translated by Rev. Jin Sakai and Jonathan Watts

"Anti-Nukes" Remains Fixed on Life: Declarations from the Religious World Come One after Another

Kyoko Isa

Up until now, it could not be said that the religious world had actively confronted the nuclear problem in Japan. Now, however, declarations aimed at nuclear society are coming one after another. There are appeals coming from the standpoint of "life" that are drawing a line at the problems of energy, environment, and local economics.

On December 1st, the Japan Buddhist Federation (JBF)—an association of 104 traditional sects and denominations from all over the country—assembled its representatives and made a joint reflection on the issue. They then adopted a declaration that stated in part, "We will strive to reduce our dependence on such nuclear power that threatens life". Rev. Yoshiharu Tomatsu, who acts as the present Secretary General, explains that, "In the end, we need to eliminate all nuclear power. We make this appeal as Buddhists." This is the first time that JBF has raised its voice about nuclear power.

The Myoshin-ji sect of the Rinzai Zen denomination has also made a public declaration stating, "We must break away at once from dependence on nuclear power for the future of our children"; and "In Buddhism, there is taught the practice of 'sufficiency' *(chisoku, samstuti/ santuthi)*, and we must make an effort to create a sustainable symbiotic society." The Zen Study Group of Eihei-ji, the main temple of the Soto Zen denomination in Fukui Prefecture, sponsored a symposium on the theme, "The Way to Live without Choosing Nuclear Power"; and so a movement is being born. Further, on November 8, the Japan Catholic Pontifical Council released a statement calling on the immediate discontinuation of all nuclear power within Japan.

Rev. Hiroaki Osada is the abbot of Hoten-ji, a Pure Land Jodo Shin Otani denomination temple in Hyogo Prefecture. Being active in the anti-nuclear movement for some time now, he guards over some complicated memories. In 1993, he was part of a group that created the Inter Faith Forum for the Review of National Nuclear Policy, which now consists of 800 members. They are religious leaders from Buddhist, Shinto, and Christian backgrounds who for many years all over Japan have made appeals concerning the nuclear issue. In the wake of the Fukushima incident, they all felt crestfallen that, "If we had just had more power, we could have stopped this incident from happening." The Forum was created at the time of the first trials of the Monju Fast Breeder Reactor built in Fukui Prefecture. Since then, they have spoken out on religious leaders' responsibility to point out the problem of the national nuclear energy policy and called for changes in the policy. However, within the religious world, this is a small faction.

Rev. Osada was born in a temple in Ishikawa Prefecture, just north of Fukui Prefecture on the Japan Sea. It is a region that had been called a "Jodo Shin Kingdom" because of the history of powerful resistance movements led by Shin priests and followers called *ikko ikki* in the 15th and 16th centuries. In 1989 and 1993 during the election for the mayor of Suzu City, the pros and cons of building a nuclear power plant in the region became a point of contention, and the community of believers was torn in two over whether to endorse it or not. The faction that opposed the plant—called the "Association of the Jodo Shin Otani Denomination in Noto Opposed to Nuclear Power" created by Rev. Osada—made the following criticism, "There are those priests who say that the problems of this *saha* world are not Buddha dharma. Are you really fellow Shin priests?" The Otani headquarters subsequently forbade the group to use the denomination's name for the association and made a statement that, "Religious leaders who engage in political activities are undesirable."

Rev. Osada notes that, "After the defeat of the *ikko ikki* movement, the Otani denomination supported the Tokugawa Era class system, and then during the Meiji Era, it separated religious issues from real life and preached belief in the 'Empire'." From this basis, Rev. Osada points out that, "The perception developed that there was no use in opposing 'His Highness' (the Emperor) or that nothing that 'His Highness' did could be wrong. This is the incredibly deep rooted background of the acceptance of nuclear power."

In 1999 when a critical nuclear incident took place at Tokaimura in Ibaraki Prefecture, the Otani denomination raised a voice to appeal for the review of the national energy policy, and Rev. Osada published a booklet that he edited called "Nuclear Power Steals Away Life." However, this did not lead the denomination to make an anti-nuclear declaration since the Fukushima nuclear incident. During this period, Rev. Osada has been receiving successive requests from civil society groups and temples all over the country to give lectures. The members of the Inter Faith Forum for the Review of National Nuclear Policy published in 2001 a book detailing the reality of these nuclear power villages and towns called *The Danger of Widespread Nuclear Contamination* (Yugaku Publishing), which is being re-edited after ten years. Rev. Osada hopes that, "With the voice of JBF, if every denomination became active, it could become very powerful."

Translated by Jonathan Watts
from the Asahi Shimbun
December 12, 2011

A Futuristic Priest Whose Time Has Arrived: Rev. Hidehito Okochi

By Jonathan Watts

He has established a micro-credit "Future Bank", is developing buildings and houses to last 100 years, and is now working for a nuclear free Japan to "recover hope within 300 years". Rev. Hidehito Okochi is a forward-looking Japanese Buddhist priest who has been ahead of the times for years. However, with the tsunami disaster of March 11 and the ongoing Fukushima nuclear reactor crisis, *his time* has arrived. Rev. Okochi has been a "socially engaged Buddhist" from his teens as a student activist and his 20s helping establish a Japanese Buddhist NGO for overseas aid work. What has differentiated him from most other engaged Buddhists in Japan up to this time has been his commitment to go beyond social welfare to social transformation. Working to transform his own community as much as engaging in overseas work, his agenda has often been too radical for most other Japanese Buddhist priests to understand or to join in. However, the political struggle over the collusion between the government and the national electric companies and the debate over the future of the country's energy policy flows right into Rev. Okochi's long held analysis of Japanese society and his vision for reforming society based on Buddhist values.

The Radical of the Second Noble Truth: Structural Suffering

Rev. Okochi, like most Japanese priests, was born in a temple and raised to succeed his father as abbot. However, instead of entering the Buddhist Studies Department of the university affiliated with his Jodo Pure Land denomination, he entered the Law and Political Science Department of the prestigious Keio University. Growing up in the late 1960s and early 1970s, Rev. Okochi was strongly influenced by the Japanese student political movement of the era; a movement that is for the most part dead today. Still, his ties to his family temple and his subsequent ordination as a priest, led him to search for the common points in his socio-political interests and his Buddhist path. He says, "Eventually I made the connection between the student movement ideals for political peace with Buddhist values for peace and social justice like no poverty and no discrimination. I also eventually saw how environment was connected to peace, and how I could work for society as a priest."

In his 20s, he and a group of other like-minded Buddhist priests took several trips abroad to various regions of conflict, especially war torn Indo-China. These intimate encounters with the suffering of humanity led them to create AYUS, a Japanese Buddhist NGO focused on supporting small NGOs doing aid work in these areas. At this time, other Japanese Buddhist priests were developing similar concerns and a group of successful, overseas aid Buddhist NGOs sprouted up and continue their work today. [1]

However, these initiatives were not enough to satisfy Rev. Okochi's political sensibilities for social justice. Reflecting on the Buddha's Four Noble Truths, Rev. Okochi went deeper into the nature of the suffering that he had encountered overseas.

> When Shakyamuni Buddha gained enlightenment, his first teaching was the Four Noble Truths, that is: first, get a solid grasp of the suffering (the problem); second, ascertain its causes and structure; third, form an image of the world to be aimed for; and fourth, act according to correct practices. From this, one gains a sense of the meaning of life in modern society as a citizen with responsibilities in the irreversible course of time. The suffering of the southern peoples and nature, from which we derive support for our lives even as we exploit it, has caused the Edogawa Citizens Network for Thinking about Global Warming (ECNG) to think, and therefore we have achieved concrete results. The problem is structural in nature, so by changing the system and creating measures for improvement, we achieve results. The first thing is to fulfill our responsibilities to the people around us and to future generations. [2]

---

[1] Watts, Jonathan S. A Brief Overview of Buddhist NGOs in Japan. *Japanese Journal of Religious Studies* 31 (2): 417–28, 2004.

[2] Okochi, Hidehito. "The Citizen's Strategy for Creating a New World: The Future Starts with Us". *New Internationalist Japan*. No. 30, Jan-Feb. 2002. http://www.ni-japan.com/webold/jbody342.htm. Also on the Juko-in homepage: http://www.juko-in.or.jp/Eactivity.htm#sokuon

Rev. Okochi discovered that the Japanese economic prosperity of the 1980s was built on the back of the economic and environmental exploitation of South and Southeast Asia while piggy backing on the political exploitation of the United States in the Middle East. While other Buddhist priests may have also seen this second noble truth, almost all have been content in working on the first noble truth of immediate suffering through social welfare and aid work overseas. Rev. Okochi has been a pioneer in the Buddhist world of Japan for not only engaging in activist and advocacy campaigns on these issues within Japan, such as his leadership of the Palestinian Children's Campaign. More importantly, he has engaged in his own community to end the complicity with this overseas exploitation rooted in Japanese consumeristic lifestyles.

The critical consciousness developed in understanding the global system of economic, environmental, and political exploitation from engaging in the second noble truth led Rev. Okochi to the third noble truth. His endeavor to create a future vision of Japan comes from his own Buddhist ideals and values. He has drawn heavily on the founder of his Jodo Pure Land denomination, Honen (1133-1212). Honen brought Japanese Buddhism down to the masses by developing a faith based in the vow of Amida Buddha to abandon no sentient being no matter how deep their transgressions and defilements. For Rev. Okochi, this means creating a world without discrimination and exploitation, especially one without a military and nuclear presence. In this way, Rev. Okochi has been part of a group of farsighted Japanese religious leaders who formed the Inter Faith Forum for the Review of National Nuclear Policy in 1993.

Acting Locally and Nurturing Community through Concern for Global Warming

The second aspect of his vision derived from Honen is nurturing community based on trusting relationships and self-reliance. This was an endeavor he set about working on in his urban temple community in Tokyo through supporting and hosting a wide variety of NGOs in a building owned by his Juko-in temple. In one large office space are found:

- a children's theatre group
- an indigenous Japanese peoples' (Ainu) advocacy group
- an environmental group for keeping the nearby Arakawa River and its environs clean
- a small political party with numerous woman candidates
- an alternative energy and culture NGO supporting the peoples of northern India called Julay Ladakh
- a micro-credit bank called Mirai (Future) Bank
- the aforementioned Edogawa Citizen's Network for Thinking about Global Warming (ECNG).

These are further integrated with a host of other citizens groups located in the area in what is called the Edogawa Lifestyle Network. In this way, Rev. Okochi has sought to connect the people in his neighborhood together on important local issues and then connect them to peoples with similar concerns in other parts of the world towards building "global community".

ECNG is an important lynchpin for the wide swath of Rev. Okochi's efforts. It was established in the summer of 1996 in the run-up to the Third Session of the Conference of the Parties to the United Nations Framework Convention on Climate Change (COP3) held in Kyoto in December 1997, resulting in the Kyoto Protocol. ECNG members started learning about global warming by first engaging in the recovery of CFCs in their local ward, which is responsible for 60% of such emissions in the central Tokyo 23 ward area due to its high concentration of car demolition businesses. This project led into a deeper investigation of Japan's industrial grid and the generation of electricity. Rev. Okochi explains that:

> In Japan, [electrical] power is held by businesses wanting to proceed with multi-billion-dollar projects at any cost, regions looking for grant money, and politicians using large amounts of political funding enticed by incentives of several percent ... [Therefore], ECNG has made it a goal not only to reduce peak [electricity] demand and change policy in order to promote the spread of alternative forms of energy, but also

to familiarize people with the concept of energy and get communities involved in initiatives … The first test of this was the establishment of the citizens' power plant using solar electrical generation.[3]

The site for this "plant" was none other than Rev. Okochi's Juko-in temple, and this required a complete rebuilding of the 400-year old temple using eco-friendly concrete and wood building materials. Two sets of fifteen large solar panels with an output of 5.4kw were installed on the roof of the newly constructed temple in 1999. It is estimated that 3kw is enough to meet the needs for the activities of a family of four, so the plant produces a little less than twice that. This initiative was an experiment not in creating an alternative form of large-scale electrical generation but in how an individual home could develop sustainable electrical independence.

Rev. Okochi points out that the big obstacle was the six million yen cost of installing the panels. The electricity generated is used primarily by Juko-in temple, and due to laws that prevent the sale of surplus electricity directly to citizens—another example of the collusion between the government and large electric companies to control the industry—Rev. Okochi has to sell it back to the Tokyo Electric Power Company, the same company that manages the Fukushima reactors. Rev. Okochi notes:

> If only the portion used by Juko-in temple and that sold to Tokyo Electric Power Co. are considered as returns, it would take fifteen years or more to pay off the initial investment, so we decided to issue Green Power Certificates. In Europe and other places, there are regions that stipulate the obligation to buy natural energy—which does not put a cost burden on the future by harming the environment or creating radioactive waste—at a higher price than that of energy generated by normal means. There are also green power systems, which designate power produced by consumers using clean generation methods and purchase it at higher prices.[4]

---

[3] Okochi. "The Citizen's Strategy for Creating a New World".

[4] Okochi. "The Citizen's Strategy for Creating a New World".

As Rev. Okochi further explains, ECNG decided to sell these Green Power Certificates to pay for the annual generation of 6000 kWh by the First Edogawa Citizens' Power Plant located at Juko-in temple at the price of ¥33/kWh, a figure between the ¥22/kWh price paid by Tokyo Electric Power Co. and the ¥55/kWh price paid for natural energy in Germany. By selling 200 certificates at ¥1,000 each, they reduced the time for return on investment to within nine years. ECNG then created a local currency called Edogawatt and provided three 10 unit Edogawatt bills for each certificate to use in exchange for baby-sitting, carrying loads, translating, and other small jobs within the community. Rev. Okochi points out that these "have provided an incentive for the creation of a mutual aid society within the community, and we would like to make them a tool for deepening interpersonal relationships and trust."[5]

The fulcrum for this whole initiative was the Mirai "Future" Bank ECNG established based on the micro credit banking systems first developed in Sri Lanka by the well known Buddhist based Sarvodaya Shramadana Movement under A.T. Ariyaratne and made famous by the Grameen Bank and Nobel Peace Prize Winner Muhammad Yunus in Bangladesh. The bank provided an important amount of capital for installing the solar panels on the roof of Juko-in and for the subsequent power station of 3kw built in 2007 on the roof of an elderly home run by a local NGO on land owned by the temple. The bank also engaged in a consumer campaign to decrease the amount of electricity used through the purchase of more energy efficient, electrical appliances. In the end, they discovered that with almost a tenth of the six million yen investment for solar panels on the roof on Juko-in used towards such appliances and products, they could save 2,000 kwH more than these panels could generate in a year. In this way, through both generating their own electricity and saving on the electricity they do use, Juko-in temple has become a successful model for realizing the final vision of every home becoming totally energy self-sufficient—thereby empowering it to unplug from centralized electrical grids.

---

[5] Okochi. "The Citizen 's Strategy for Creating a New World".

Rebuilding Local Resources, Local Ecology, and Local Community

This initiative feeds into a larger vision Rev. Okochi has for developing a pure land here on earth through ecological housing and living. Rev. Okochi has joined together with a host a different small Japanese NGOs to build chemical free, long lasting homes for urban dwellers. In his first experiences in Southeast Asia and through a study tour of Sarawak, Malaysia with ECNG, he came to learn of large Japanese companies, like Mitsubishi, which engage in destructive logging practices, while local timber companies within Japan have gone out of business. Not only has this been destroying the forests of Southeast Asia, but the abandoned mono-culture forests planted in previous years by local companies within Japan are now causing soil erosion, landslides, and a host of local environmental problems.

The vision Rev. Okochi and his partners developed is part of the increasingly well-known Japanese *sato-yama* (village-mountain) policy for developing sustainable human communities living in co-existence with forests as well as marine environments *(sato-umi)*. The plan has been to replant Japan's forests in consultation with marginalized, traditional Japanese architects and carpenters with a variety of hardwoods that will enrich biological diversity, avoid soil erosion, and provide a sustainable supply of timber for construction use. Most houses that are built today by major contractors in Japan use heavy amounts of chemicals leading to the phenomenon known as "sick houses" for the respiratory, skin, and other problems they cause new inhabitants. Further, they are made of cheap monoculture timbers that last only one generation. This eco-village initiative is to build houses that last three generations with natural materials that increase the well-being of their inhabitants.

Another crucial aspect of these initiatives is support for the development of local electrical generation through the use of solar, wind, and micro-hydroelectric. As Rev. Okochi points out, the myth that Japan has no natural resources is part of the larger myth of the need for massive centralized electrical systems—including nuclear power—to fuel an exploitative, consumer driven economy. Again, Rev. Okochi has lived this vision by completely rebuilding a second temple for which he serves as abbot. Kenju-in temple is located in downtown Tokyo with four floors of chemical free, low cost apartments for urban dwellers with environmental values.

All these initiatives are what Rev. Okochi believes can lead Japan away from a top down, oil dependent society, which in turn must support American militarism to support oil security. While the Japanese government, like many other governments, has used the promise of nuclear power to distance itself from oil dependency and fulfill targets to reducing green house gas emissions, nuclear power has been a means to reinforce a top down social order that ensures the profits of electric companies and their "associates", exploits laborers in the plants, and robs communities in remote regions of their independence while endangering their future. Rev. Okochi's notes that his vision of and practices towards a natural energy society would "reverse the social hierarchy" by decentralizing the production and consumption of energy and empowering localities and individuals to better determine their own futures.

Conclusion

Since the triple disaster of March 11, Rev. Okochi's Inter Faith Forum for the Review of National Nuclear Policy has been busy offering their churches, temples, and other facilities as shelters for families who want to evacuate the areas around the Fukushima nuclear power plant. They have also continued their advocacy work writing a series of ongoing editorials in the Japanese Buddhist newspapers and giving public talks all over the country. They hope to expand their advocacy work internationally by participating in the first inter-Buddhist dialogue on climate change to be held in September 2012 in Sri Lanka by the International Network of Engaged Buddhists (INEB), a group Rev. Okochi has been active in for the last three years.

Before March 11, Rev. Okochi was already supporting the dissemination of Helena Norberg-Hodge's film *The Economics of Happiness,* which points directly at the problems now facing Japanese society from years of following an exploitative, consumerist economy.

At a showing of this movie in June at his alma mater Keio University, Rev. Okochi was struck by the political apathy to these issues, especially the nuclear one, by today's university students—although many of the "drop out" youth in Japan have been heavily involved in the nuclear protests. He feels that more than being apathetic, today's young "educated" Japanese seem ignorant of important social issues. They are so consumed by their own career paths and by the internet and other forms of social entertainment that they do not seem to have time for being concerned about social issues. It is to this ignorance, the root cause of all suffering as the Buddha taught, that Rev. Okochi has been spending his life addressing. Unwilling to stay ignorant to the second noble truth, he has been building a future in Japan that may hopefully be arriving sooner than expected.

PART III

MESSAGES FROM INTERNATIONAL
BUDDHIST LEADERS ON THE FUTURE
OF JAPAN

Message to the Japanese People from The World Fellowship of Buddhists

March 16, 2011

With so many troubles affecting the stability and peace of the world, many of which are based on materialistic gains, such an overwhelmingly heartbreaking natural disaster of unprecedented proportions starkly reminds us that we are all of the same vulnerable human family. It is impossible to not be shocked and deeply distressed to witness the destruction of homes, industries, infrastructure, and most importantly the lives and wellbeing of our extended global families.

Our emotions of overwhelming concern and sympathy are unreservedly extended to the families who have lost loved ones; and to the injured, we wish that they will receive all necessary support towards their earliest recovery. The affects will be felt for a long time, and we are compelled to extend our compassionate support in any way that we can to ensure that the terrible situation is not born alone by our Japanese friends.

In times of immense crisis and human distress, there are no divisions of race, religion, or culture—just grandparents, mothers and fathers, husbands and wives, brothers and sisters, children, babies and people; people that are as real as our very own beloved family members and friends. Please know that the sorrow of the Japanese Nation is shared in the saddest of contemplation by all members of the World Fellowship of Buddhists and all compassionate people around the world.

The world's reaction of shock, including messages of sympathy and condolences combined with practical assistance, has clearly indicated that humankind has not lost the ability to love and care for one and other, reaching out with the hand of comfort, aid, and support in times of need. On many occasions in history the Japanese Nation has faced great difficulties and suffering, on each occasion estimably displaying their fortitude and practical ability to overcome and in due course prosper. It is our sincere wish that the following period to full recovery will be as short as possible.

With globalisation, the nations of the world are entwined in such a way that the pain of one nation is felt by all. This disaster is a disaster for all human beings. Also, offering our most sincere condolences for all losses of life, we join with the Japanese people in their sorrow, prayers, and efforts to deal with the enormous challenges that are to be faced and overcome.

With the utmost concern and respect, yours in the Dharma,
Phan Wannamethee
President - The World Fellowship of Buddhists

Engaged Buddhism the Dalai Lama's Way: Tibetan Leader's Exceptional Energy for Japan's Tsunami Victims

Jonathan Watts

His Holiness the Dalai Lama has shown exceptional energy towards the Japanese people over the past year, and especially to the victims of the March 11th tsunami disaster. On the first day after the disasters, he issued a public statement offering his prayers and condolences to the people of Japan. He also offered spiritual advice recommending the frequent chanting of the *Prajnaparamita Heart Sutra*. As a Buddhist monk and someone who recites the *Heart Sutra* daily, the Dalai Lama stated that recitation of the *Heart Sutra* would not only be helpful for those who had perished in the disaster but may also help prevent further disasters in the future. In addition to encouraging everyone in the Tibetan communities worldwide to pray for and chant the *Heart Sutra* for the Japanese people, he organized recitation of the *Heart Sutra* one hundred thousand times at the main temple near the Tibetan Government in Exile's headquarters in Dharamsala, India.

While many other world leaders and Buddhist leaders offered such condolences, the Dalai Lama was the first to make a special trip to Japan to offer greater encouragement to the Japanese. He made a special diversion from his planned trip to the United States to come to Tokyo while the nuclear incident in Fukushima was unfolding and many other social, political, and religious personalities were cancelling their visits to Tokyo. Exemplifying an engaged Buddhist, the Dalai Lama did not recoil or back down from the danger, fear, and suffering, but rather chose to actively encounter it.

Special Memorial and Consoling Service on the 49th Day after the Tsunami

April 29th marked the 49th day since the disaster. In Buddhism, this day is considered the critical final day for a deceased's consciousness to remain wandering in the intermediate state *(bardo/chuin)* before taking rebirth. The Dalai Lama presided over a special memorial service at Gokoku-ji Temple in Tokyo on this day for those who perished in the earthquake and tsunami. The 40-minute service included 15 Tibetan monks and 100 Japanese priests and nuns from a variety of sects, including the abbot of Soto Zen's second main temple Sojo-ji and the abbot of Gokoku-ji, a head temple of the Shingon Koyasan sect. They chanted the *Heart Sutra* for extended periods in both Tibetan and Japanese. A gathering public from a wide variety of backgrounds numbering around 3,000 stuffed into the main hall and filled the compound outside, watching the service on three large television monitors.

After the ceremony, the Dalai Lama gave an address in Tibetan in which he offered his deepest condolences to the Japanese people over the suffering caused by the March 11 events. He then gave another address in English in which he encouraged the Japanese as follows:

> During World War II, there was a lot of destruction and many Japanese were killed. Two nuclear bombs were dropped on Hiroshima and Nagasaki, but our Japanese brothers and sisters never lost their self-confidence … Now you are passing through some difficulties, including economic difficulties, but you must keep your self-confidence. Instead of remembering this tragedy and the loss of friends and always being reminded of the sad situation, now move forward. You have the potential. So work hard.

He then offered a more nuanced message on this way forward:

> Now due to global warming, this kind of natural disaster may come often, so you must work to prevent it. But there is no guarantee. Things are changing. You must look at the new

reality and act according to that reality, for example about your lifestyle. Sometimes, in much developed countries, they live a very luxurious life. According to our new situation and obviously on this planet, that is silly. Millions and millions of people live in extreme lifestyles under poverty. The last few years when I have the opportunity to be with Japanese friends, particularly students, I urge them to learn English. This is so you can use your potential in different parts of the world for more constructive purposes in the educational field, the health field, and the development or technology fields. The Japanese people have a big population and a small amount of land, so every piece of land you utilize fully; whereas in some other big countries there is a lot of empty land. You must utilize your experience and expertise for how to utilize wasted land and wasted resources without damaging the ecology. That is what I want to share with you.

After concluding this address, he proceeded out of the main hall and toward to the temple's main bell in the main courtyard. Ascending into the bell tower, he rang the bell numerous times himself in a sign of traditional mourning. Finally, he slowly waded through the crowd stopping to talk to various people on the way to his vehicle and finally departed into the afternoon sun. The event was special in that not only was it covered well by the mass media, which usually shows no interest in Buddhist ceremonies in Japan, but also was attended by a wide variety of people offering an uncommon feeling of non-sectarianism and public outpouring of religiosity in this very secularized country. The Dalai Lama's visit served not only to support the healing of Japan after the disaster but, as always, offered a point of common humanity and spirituality to bond people of various backgrounds together.

Visits to the Tsunami Areas in November

Some six months later, the Dalai Lama made a longer extended visit to Japan focusing on interacting with the people in the disaster areas. On November 5th, the Dalai Lama journeyed to Sendai City and its environs in Miyagi Prefecture. In the morning, he visited the Jodo Pure Land temple of Saiko-ji in the hard hit city of Ishinomaki to hold a prayer service for the revival of the community. The site of Saiko-ji, with Hiyoriyama mountain in the background, became inundated with massive amounts of debris at the time of the tsunami. One part of the temple was destroyed, and there was sludge remaining in the main hall that had to be scraped out as much as possible. By November, the debris had been totally cleared away and the cleaned up environs of the temple held special seats for residents to watch over the prayer service.

Children from the nearby kindergarten and other victims warmly greeted the Dalai Lama with palms together. The Dalai Lama exchanged warm embraces with the children and greeted people holding framed pictures of loved ones who had perished in the disaster. During the prayer service for the revival of the area, there was a chanting of the *Heart Sutra* by a group of local priests from various denominations, which was then followed by a group of accompanying Tibetan monks chanting the sutra in Tibetan.

During his subsequent talk, the Dalai Lama tried to encourage the victims by recounting his own experiences overcoming the difficulties at the time of his exile from Tibet and coming in contact with the revival in Hiroshima and Nagasaki after World War II. He said, "All you Japanese are courageous and diligent and have the character of helping each other out. You have the power of truly wonderful hearts and I think you can certainly restore this beautiful city."[1] He then commented, "As humans, we have intelligence. When such a thing happens, we must think. With our intelligence, combined with self-confidence, we can overcome all these problems. So tragedy certainly, naturally, brings sadness and demoralizes us; but now you must transform it into enthusiasm and self-confidence and work hard to rebuild your lives, your country. Particularly with these young children here: provide them with education and let them lead another happy new generation." [2]

The Dalai Lama then moved on to Sendai to the Nichiren temple of Kosho-ji, where he gave another prayer service for community

---

[1] "Darai rama juyonse-ga hisai-chi hairi, hisai-sha-to chokusetsu fure-ai gekirei" (The 14th Dalai Lama enters the disaster areas and directly meets victims and encourages them) *Bukkyo Times*. November 10, 2011. Translation by author.

[2] The Transformation of Pain. Website of His Holiness the 14th Dalai Lama of Tibet. November 5, 2011. http://www.dalailama.com/news/post/762-the-transformation-of-pain

revival and a public talk sponsored by the Buddhist Association of Sendai. In the morning, he had developed an emotional connection with the audience and spoke more from the heart. Here, in the afternoon, he gave a more analytical and practical talk of how to use Buddhist teachings to look at suffering realistically and transform it into possibility.[3] He presented the teaching of "voidness" *(sunnata/ku)* as a way of not getting stuck in negative feelings, noting, "We tend to bring greater suffering to ourselves when we believe that we have a fundamental self that must experience fundamental suffering." One person in the audience asked, "What should one do when unhappiness suddenly springs forth?" The Dalai Lama further explained that, "One can even make use of the path of hardship for achieving enlightenment ... By using the fact that things arise and fall, the way we deal with suffering can change as well as our thinking about the essence of suffering." A final important message he gave was: "It is not about forgetting suffering, but rather the fact that the 'state' of suffering changes." [4]

Approximately 2,500 people attended at each of these temples and listened attentively to his powerful message of revival. In a country that has become largely urban and secular, losing contact with its Buddhist roots, the outpouring of feeling at these events and the connection His Holiness made with the people—like during the event in Tokyo in April—was truly remarkable for a public religious event in Japan. It also showed to the country the still strong faith and connection that Japanese in the less urban areas of the Northeast have towards Buddhism.

Wrestling with the Nuclear Issue

Before returning to Tokyo and leaving the country, the Dalai Lama made a stop in Fukushima Prefecture on November 6th to give a talk at Nihon University in Koriyama City, some 60 kms from the crippled nuclear power plants. Although this is 40 kms from the no entry zone, a radiation reading taken in the middle of the city just before the Tibetan leader's arrival showed a reading of 2.28 microsievert/hour—a mark dangerously bordering the radiation level considered hazardous for human life if continuously exposed for a year.[5] The Dalai Lama said

---

[3] The Transformation of Pain

[4] *Bukkyo Times*. November 10, 2011.

[5] Woeser, Sherab. "The Dalai Lama braves radiation threat, Interacts with victims." *Phayul*. November 6, 2011. http://www.phayul.com/news/article.aspx?id=30337

at his talk, "More natural disasters might come in the future because of global warming, so it is better you move to higher grounds and rebuild your home and family with greater enthusiasm".[6]

It was this continuous engagement with the suffering of the Japanese people—which took the Dalai Lama to areas considered unsafe in Tokyo in April and in Koriyama in November—that led to surprise during a news conference in Tokyo on his final official day in Japan November 7th. At this press conference, the Dalai Lama, when asked a question about nuclear energy, did not condemn it. His comments caused enough of a controversy in the media that the Liaison Office of the Dalai Lama for Japan and East Asia located in Tokyo issued the following official statement on November 15th:

Statement by His Holiness the Dalai Lama on Nuclear Energy [7]

On November 7th, at a reporters meeting of the Free Press Association of Japan in Tokyo, there was a question concerning His Holiness' stance on nuclear power by one reporter who then stated, "The Dalai Lama said that he endorses nuclear energy." As this is a misunderstanding based on one part of His Holiness' view concerning nuclear power, we would like to make the following public statement to communicate a proper understanding of the His Holiness' views to everyone. – Liaison Office of H.H. the Dalai Lama for Japan and East Asia

First of all, in the case of any issue, it is not proper to jump to a conclusion based on one viewpoint or perspective. It is important to develop a complete way of understanding by grasping an issue from a variety of perspectives.

Concerning nuclear energy, the use of it for destructive purposes creates a great disaster. I myself have visited Hiroshima many times. On the first or second time, I saw the buildings on which the bomb was dropped that were totally destroyed. I also visited the Hiroshima Peace Memorial Museum and saw the display of the wristwatch of a survivor that had been burned and melted to the exact time of the dropping of the bomb. I also visited some of the victims who had been contaminated

---

[6] Woeser, Sherab

[7] After being unable to locate an English version on His Holiness' official homepage, this statement was translated by the author from the Japanese site of the Liaison Office of H.H. the Dalai Lama for Japan and East Asia http://www.tibethouse.jp/news_release/2011/111115_nuclear.html

by the radiation and listened to their truly tragic stories. In this way, I myself am absolutely against the use of nuclear weapons.

On the issue of nuclear energy being used for peaceful means, if there is a sufficient substitute for nuclear energy and we could therefore do away with it completely, I think that would be wonderful. However, there is still room for debate. If we think about substitutes, hydropower necessitates dams, of which there are in my homeland of Tibet. Because the construction of dams has been connected to tremendous environmental destruction, I cannot support their promotion. Wind power and solar power have still not yet been developed enough. In this way, I think we must consider the millions of people living in poverty and the severe gap between the rich and poor, not in developed countries like Japan, but in the many still economically developing countries in the world.

Therefore, we need to have the judgment of real experts who can analyze the matter comprehensively. In this way, if a conceived measure is 99% flawless, we can say it is safe. But then there is still a 1% danger remaining. Even in driving an automobile, or eating wonderful food, or being in what appears to be a safe room, you can never know what kind of unforeseeable thing will arise. Nuclear power is the same. For example, the Chernobyl nuclear reactor had become an out of date facility that did not have proper safety measures. This time during the Fukushima nuclear incident, if someone had designed the reactors with proper safety measures based on the possibility of such a huge tsunami, then it seems such a terrible disaster would not have occurred. However, even if that measure had been taken, there still could have been a 1% chance of it happening.

In the end, it is really up to the voice of the people of a country to decide. If the Japanese people want to completely withdraw from the use of nuclear power, then that's great. I think that is the case with all peoples. In the way Germany and Italy decided to end nuclear power in their countries through a popular vote, if the Japanese have such an aspiration, that is totally fine.

Conclusion

The Dalai Lama has spent much of his public life in exile campaining tirelessly for non-violent political action and environmental conservation.

He has not been a follower on these issues, but has been a leader who has studied to understand the issues deeply and proclaimed courageous positions. In his comments above, it seems that his concerns for poverty and the violence caused by exploitative economic systems (another of his concerns) trumps the environmental and politica implications of nuclear power. Yet his comments from his talk at Gokoku-ji in Tokyo in April challenging the Japanese to adjust their lifestyles and not damage the ecology seem to be a tacit attack on the development of nuclear power and consumer lifestyles in Japan.

On the one hand, the Dalai Lama finds himself balancing his work in the conventional political realm with his role of Buddhist monk. Some think that his position on nuclear power follows the Indian government's stance on promoting nuclear energy as a fulcrum for economic growth and the so-called eradication of poverty that such growth would entail. The fallacies of this belief have been well documented, and we are thus required to consider the reasons for the Dalai Lama taking such a position. Indeed, the Dalai Lama' position may reflect the precarious position of the Tibetans as refugees, in that the Tibetan leader does not want to stir the ire of their generous host, the pro-nuclear Indian government.

On the other hand, his position on this issue seems to contrast that taken by many progressive Buddhists around the world, who consider him one of their leaders, and even the position traditionally conservative Japanese Buddhist denominations are beginning to adopt. The ongoing incident at the Fukushima nuclear facility has exposed the fallacy of nuclear power as an alternative to carbon fuels in the battle against global warming. This incident has also exposed the motives of certain Japanese politicians to use nuclear technology as a means of arming Japan with nuclear weapons [8] —an unthinkable scenario after the experiences of Hiroshima and Nagasaki and an issue that the Dalai Lama has spoken out against numerous times.[9] While many progressive Buddhists and social activists in Japan are deeply disappointed in the Dalai Lama' statement following a most heartwarming visit to Japan, a deep respect and gratitude still exists among the Japanese for the Dalai Lama' continuing care and support.

---

[8] For example, former Prime Minister Yasuhiro Nakasone. Suzuki, Takuya. "Nuclear Leverage: Long an advocate of nuclear energy, Nakasone now says Japan should go solar." *Asahi Shimbun*. July 22, 2011.

[9] For example, http://www.dalailama.com/news/post/25-dalai-lama-calls-for-nuclear-free-world

No More Back to Business as Usual: A Socially Engaged Buddhist Approach to Making a Post 3/11 Society in Japan

Sulak Sivaraksa

---

*S*ulak Sivaraksa is a renowned Thai author, social critic, and spiritual activist. Among the many social and spiritual development NGOs he founded in his native Siam (Thailand), he helped to found the International Network of Engaged Buddhists (INEB) in 1989. In July, 2011, he became the 29th recipient of the Niwano Peace Prize for his lifetime work. This essay is based on a talk given at Kenju-in, the temple of Rev. Hidehito Okochi, in Tokyo on July 26, 2011.

Introduction

The events of March 11th are something very significant. I think people should take them seriously, which means we should not return to business as usual. People in power either in the political, economic, or scientific spheres think they can change and improve things, so they never seem to learn from crisis. The cause of 3/11 in fact comes from human arrogance. We think we can control nature and invent something supremely powerful. Now nature has shown to us repeatedly that it is beyond human control and imagination. I think it is time we learn to become humble and to respect nature and other human beings.

After Japan was forced to open itself to the West in the mid 1800s, they began to follow the West. After their victory in the Russo-Japanese War of 1904-05, they began to feel they could compete with the West and master scientific and technological knowledge no less than the West. The disaster at Fukushima shows they have not really learned that western successes also constitute their failures. In this way, I think perhaps the Japanese have been uprooted from their wonderful nature. Although most people consider the Japanese to be Buddhist, I think they have been alienated from the essential teaching of the Buddha.

In Buddhism, the first thing one learns is how to be humble and respectful. In the modern West, however, the first thing we learn is how to be arrogant and to compete with others. I think there is a great difference here. In the Theravada Buddhist tradition to which I belong, we are told that we will be blessed with life force, good health, and strength (mental, spiritual and physical), provided we remain humble and respectful to those who are to be respected, such as our parents, elders, nature, and all natural phenomena. In the Thai language, we call the river, "mother water"; the earth, "mother earth"; and the rice, "mother rice". I think this is a wonderful sign of how we respect mother nature. In the modern West, nature is regarded as natural resources to be exploited. People like St. Francis of Assisi who preached to animals and took other sentient beings seriously in the 13th century is not in the mainstream. I think it is about time we Asians learn to come back to our roots and seriously question western civilization.

Humility from the Buddhist point of view is that you learn to tame the ego. The ego tends to be oppressive, but humility tames and reduces the ego. It teaches you not to take the ego seriously. This is the first step in training. Once you learn that your own self is not that important, you learn to serve others. Other human beings as sentient beings are more important than you. This is the idea of Buddhism towards life, nature, and sentient beings. The more you want to promote your own happiness, the more selfish you become and the more you end up in suffering. The more you try to promote the happiness of others, the more you are on the right track if you do it skillfully.

In Buddhism, once you learn to become humble and respectful, then you take refuge in the Buddha, Dhamma, and Sangha. Refuge in the Buddha means that we all can become awakened. Taking refuge in the Dhamma means that we can come to the truth. Taking refuge in the Sangha means that we can live in community, equally, with fraternity in order to liberate ourselves from greed, hatred, and delusion. Nowadays we don't take refuge in the Buddha but take refuge in how to become rich, powerful, exploitative—and this makes us all unhappy.

In Theravada Buddhism, once you take refuge in the Buddha,

Dhamma, and Sangha then you take the Five Precepts *(pancasila)*. You learn not to kill, not to steal, not to make sexual offence, not to lie, and not to take intoxicants. The Five Precepts are not commandments. You are not told what to do. Rather, they are guidelines on how to live a normal life, a natural life, a life of happiness. In the first precept on not killing, we can ask, why should we not kill? When we kill, the other suffers, but the killer also suffers because he/she promotes violence. The more violent we are, the more we are not natural and not normal. In the second precept on stealing, when you steal, someone loses their property; but even for the one who steals, it is bad for you because you promote greed and again you are no longer normal, no longer natural. In the third precept regarding wrongful sexual acts, when you do that, someone else suffers and you yourself promote lust. In the fourth precept concerning lying, when you tell lies, someone does not get the truth, and you yourself begin to believe in your own lies. This is very dangerous and is why politicians and advertisers believe their own lies. The fifth precept on not taking intoxicants is basically about advising people to be mindful, not mindless. Alcohol and drugs may make you mindless, but advertizing can also make you mindless. Ideologies and even Buddhism when it is not properly taught can make you mindless.

Socially Engaged Buddhism is about Social Structures

What I have just presented is the traditional Buddhist approach, but socially engaged Buddhism has to be more meaningful this. Nowadays we don't need to kill, but we allow our government to kill. We allow the government to draft people to kill and then spend so much money on arms. I think if one is truly a committed Buddhist, one must challenge the government on no killing, no dreadful weapons, and reducing budgets on arms. In the second precept as well, we don't need to steal anymore, we just allow the banks to steal for us. The World Bank is the biggest organization stealing from the poor for the rich, and most of us are not aware of it. Rich people exploit poor people; rich nations exploit poor nations; and all nations are controlled by transnational corporations. This is stealing at the global level. I could elaborate on each precept here at greater length, but the gist of the matter is that modern social structures are so unjust, violent, and exploitative.

If a modern Buddhist does not understand social structures, I think he/she is not socially engaged—and perhaps they have become irrelevant. When I started our movement for socially engaged Buddhism with the International Network of Engaged Buddhists (INEB) in 1989, I went to the Dalai Lama for his blessing and support. I asked him to understand social structures, but he said to me, "What do you mean by social structures? I have no idea." So I told him, "The second precept about stealing refers to how the World Bank is stealing. Do you see my point?" And he said, "Yes, yes ,yes!"

However, it is not so easy to get rid of the World Bank. I am happy that I was able to have a dialogue with the Bank through the former President, James Wolfensohn. One of his senior advisors was Catherine Marshall, and she was the one who nominated me for the Niwano Peace Prize that I received this year. Mr. Wolfensohn asked me, "You say something is wrong with the World Bank, but what is your Buddhist concept of wealth". I responded that, "The Buddhist concept of wealth is to be: 1) self-reliant, 2) content, 3) generous, and 4) mindful." He then asked me, "Where is the place of money?" I said, "Money can be helpful or harmful, but on the whole it is more harmful. That is why in Theravada Buddhism, the monks are advised not to even touch money."

Nowadays, we have been told that Gross National Product (GNP) is the criteria to measure development, progress, and success. Obviously, GNP is linked directly to mainstream, so called neo-liberal economists and to capitalism and consumerism. Capitalism means that the more money or capital we have, the better. Consumerism means that the more you consume the better and that by acquiring you will become happy—but you never do become happy. For example, Japan is one of the richest countries with scientific advancements, a high GNP, but are the people happy here? Why do so many young people commit suicide in Japan? There is clearly something fundamentally wrong. The Chinese government is now competing with the American government worldwide, selling goods all over the world and becoming economically very powerful—but the Chinese people also suffer so much. They work under the worst conditions and are very exploited; all in the service of GNP.

On the other hand, Gross National Happiness (GNH) goes back to Buddhist economics—economics as if human beings mattered. If the

Chinese cared for their workers and better working conditions, they would not need to compete with the Americans. Most Chinese people in fact would be very happy, content with a civilized lifestyle and freedom. The former King of Bhutan, Jigme Singye Wangchuck, promoted this idea of GNH during his reign when Bhutan was a closed and isolated country. People were on the whole very poor but very content and Buddhistic. When I first went to Bhutan 35 years ago, there were no high rises anywhere. The capital and other towns and villages were very similar. Most people were poor together except for a very few rich ones, but even they were practicing Buddhism and were very civilized and humble. However, now that they have opened up the country, there are many high rises, and Thimpu has become an ugly place. I think that this is very dangerous and that it will be very difficult for them to carry out Gross National Happiness. People think Bhutan is a utopian Shangri-la, but it's not.

However, I still believe in GNH. I have advised the Prime Minister of Bhutan on a better education system. Even in my country, Thailand, which is much worse than Bhutan, GNH is still possible. The reason why it is possible is that even the most advanced nations feel that what they are doing now is wrong. Leading economists who have won the Noble Prize, like Amartya Sen and Joseph Stiglitz, have come out clearly stating that the GNP model will lead to the ruin of the world. The French President, Nicolas Sarkozy, now has a team of advisors on GNH. My new book, *The Wisdom of Sustainability*, was reviewed this year in the prominent British newspaper *The Independent*, and the reviewer said in the first line, "Breathe in happily, breathe out mindfully, and drop Pepsi Cola". The second line was, "The Prime Minister of Britain should read this book." Every year at Davos, Switzerland, economists, prime ministers, and finance ministers meet on how to promote economic advancement. Last year, they invited a French Buddhist monk ordained in the Tibetan tradition named Matthieu Ricard to speak on GNH. Ricard was a scientist before becoming a monk and is very articulate. I think these are all good signs that people are probing and looking for happiness, so we should all come together to look forward, beyond "business as usual".

I am hopeful but not optimistic about engaged Buddhism in Japan. Hope gives us strength to do something meaningful, while optimism leads us to think that something will be achieved easily—but it is not so in this case. My country too is in a dreadful state politically and not so well off economically. Education wise it is very backward, so I started a small NGO fifteen years ago called the Spirit in Education Movement (SEM). Mahidol University, the most prestigious university in Thailand, has asked us to help them with their professors, many who are very arrogant and fight each other like cats and dogs. We are teaching them to breathe properly, and now they are learning to become more humble and friendly. The mayor of the biggest city in Northeast Thailand called Khon Kaen has asked us to help four schools. These four are the top schools in the city which send students to university. However, the students were not happy, and the teachers were quarrelsome. For the last few years, we have been teaching them how to be happy—it is possible. Chulalongkorn University, the oldest university in Thailand, has asked us to establish a School of Wellbeing to promote GNH in association with the Buddhist Studies Center in Thimphu, Bhutan. We are also working with Buddhist monks and an NGO promoting alternative education with a spiritual component. We work very closely with Buddhist monks in Laos, a Communist country. We have worked for fifteen years in Burma, a country run by dictatorship. We have 300,000 monks in Thailand who preach on consumerism, capitalism, funeralism, and monarchism, but having just 300 monks caring for the dharma is hopeful.

The essence of engaged Buddhism is to first begin to transform ourselves from within through meditation, by which we can then restructure our consciousness to care more for others. We must bring ourselves to see and confront others who suffer. However, this is not going to those in suffering to help them or preach to them. Rather, it means to share their lifestyle, learn from them, and perhaps to work together to change the situation. I come from an elite background and I used to think I was well educated, so I thought I could go help the poor. But once I exposed myself to the poor, I felt I learned much more from them, and this humbled me.

Making a Post 3/11 Society in Japan

I wish I could say something meaningful to the farmers and people in the nuclear disaster zones near the Fukushima nuclear facility. However, since I don't know the situation well, I think it would be presumptuous and arrogant of me to advise people. I would say, though, that I admire them to stick to their roots and their land. I think that those of us who are really concerned about the victims of the nuclear disaster or the tsunami should work to become their friends, have dialogue with them, and learn from them. My friend Hisashi Nakamura, a professor at Ryukoku University, has done this by bringing in people from the disaster areas to his home to learn from them. When people are in such desperation, they need good friends, so we should go there to live with them for two to three weeks. We should learn from those people there how they could become hopeful in a very serious situation. In this way, we can restructure our consciousness and become hopeful even when facing death. The Buddha has taught us how to face death mindfully. I think this is the first essential step if you want to apply Buddhism for the world.

For those outside the disaster areas, I think they should learn that business as usual is not possible anymore. I think we have to credit Prime Minister Naoto Kan for being very concerned about the 3/11 nuclear accident. Most politicians serve vested interests and transnational corporations rather than serving the people. Most top politicians do not have "good friends". "Good friends" in Buddhism are called *kalyanamitra*, and they are the ones who tell you what you don't want to hear. Prime Ministers do not want to be told what they don't want to hear. *Kalyanamitra* are an external voice of conscience. I think it is essential that we should be his *kalyanamitra* and talk to him as good friends. With good friends supporting him, perhaps Mr. Kan will have the moral courage to not continue business as usual. However, that would mean that his colleagues will sack him even more easily, because politicians want to have business as usual.

We have to think carefully and perhaps use our heart more than our head—learn how to meditate properly. Someone said the 21st century will be the century of spirituality, otherwise it will be the end of the world. I think we need to promote spiritual strength. When 9/11 took place in the United States last decade, the American establishment never changed and resorted to violence. However, a lot of young Americans changed. They want more spirituality and more truth, not lies and hypocrisy. The Occupy Wall Street movement has been tremendous. Yet even in Norway, the safest place in the world, the place of the Nobel Peace Prize, a terrible shooting incident just happened. People need to learn that no place is safe and to confront crisis mindfully and hopefully—then everything can be overcome.

Even here in Japan where the society is regarded as so homogenous, there are some wonderful alternatives taking place; for example, this temple we are in rebuilt by Rev. Okochi with natural, non-chemical materials and used in part as affordable apartments for the people. I think other priests will follow this model, because this is the only way for Buddhism to survive in the modern world. You cannot keep being greedy, making money doing funeral services and building ostentatious temples. We have to be more serious in practicing the Buddha's teaching by being more generous. I think this is possible here in Japan and elsewhere.

Natural Disasters and Religion: In Search of an Alternative Way of Life

Dr. A. T. Ariyaratne

---

*D*r. A. T. Ariyaratne is the founder and President of the Sarvodaya Shramadana Movement in Sri Lanka, a highly acclaimed community development organization begun in the 1950s that has spread its work throughout Sri Lanka and has had far reaching influence in other parts of Asia and the world. Dr. Ariyaratne was a also a tireless campaigner for a non-violent solution to Sri Lanka's ethnic conflict. For his efforts and work, he received the 10th Niwano Peace Prize in 1992 and the Magsaysay Award in 1969. This essay was presented at the Symposium "Thinking about Natural Disasters and Religion: Looking for Another Way of Living" sponsored by the Zenseikyo Foundation & Buddhist Council for Youth and Child Welfare at Zojo-ji Temple, Tokyo on October 10, 2012.

Introduction

When the earthquake, tsunami, and the nuclear accident happened in early March, we were with you in spirit at that time. However, besides doing religious activities to give you strength to face this situation and doing meritorious activities in the name of the victims and the deceased, we were helpless to be of any concrete physical assistance because of the great distance that separates us.

I myself was born to a Buddhist family. My parents and other elders in the family were very devoted practicing Buddhists. My home was next to our temple, and from my infancy, I had the good fortune of associating with and learning from very learned and disciplined Buddhist monks. I received my primary, secondary, and higher education mostly in Buddhist schools, colleges, and universities. When I started teaching, I spent most of my teaching days in a premier Buddhist

College known as Nalanda. It is from there that the now internationally famous Sarvodaya Shramadana Movement started 53 years ago as an experiment in building a society that works for all on the teachings of the Buddha. Whatever I write will be based on the five decades old experience in translating the Buddha's teaching into development action and attempting to restructure the over 15,000 village communities of Sri Lanka. Our objective was to develop a self-governing community model integrating the spiritual, moral, cultural, social, economic, and political life of rural communities. We call this the *gram swaraj* or community self-governance model.

The Cause of Disasters

I would like to look at the theme "Natural Disasters and Religion" in the light of the Buddha Dhamma as I understand it. According to the Jataka legends, Gautama Buddha in his previous lives as the bodhisattva struggled through innumerable cycles of births and deaths and was able to find a way to end the suffering that all beings are subject to in the samsaric cycle. He did so by discovering the Four Noble Truths, namely, the Noble Truths of suffering *(dukkha)*, the cause of suffering *(samudaya)*, the cessation of suffering *(nirodha)*, and the path leading to the cessation of suffering *(magga)*. Disaster, in whatever form it comes or in whatever way it is caused, is a part of this suffering that cannot be prevented as long as we wander in the samsaric ocean. The only way to end all suffering is by attaining the supreme bliss of Nirvana.

However, if we follow the Buddha's teachings in our day to day life, with the ultimate goal of attaining Nirvana, while living a life founded on *sila* (morality), *samadhi* (concentration), and *panna* (wisdom), it is my strong conviction that as individuals we can escape from becoming victims of any kind of disaster. We learn in the Buddhist teachings the principle known as *dhammohave rakhkhathi dhammachari,* which means, "Those who conduct themselves according to the Dhamma will be protected by the Dhamma." We often hear of certain cases of people who have had miraculous escapes when others faced with the same disastrous situations perished. These are instances where the law of karma has come into effect on those who have accumulated powerful meritorious or positive karma.

In the *Abhidhamma* texts of the Pali Canon, we come across five cosmic laws *(pancha niyama dhamma)*, which function above all human-made laws. *Kamma niyama* or the law of karma is only one. There are others known as: *bija niyama*, the laws pertaining to our genes or genetic formations; *utu niyama*, the laws governing seasons and climate; *citta niyama*, the laws determining the effects of volitions on the psycho-sphere as a whole; and *dhamma niyama*, the cosmic laws that control everything else pertaining to our conduct toward one another, relationships with other living beings, and the natural world itself. When we go into deep contemplation on these five natural laws, one wonders whether most of what go under the label "natural disasters" are really caused by nature's "misconduct" or humankind's misbehavior caused by our own endless greed, aversion, and ignorance.

Some of the unfortunate disasters like earthquakes, tsunami, typhoons, floods, droughts, lightening, etc. that we attribute to nature are perhaps not brought on by nature but by humans themselves. When human beings violate the *pancha niyama dhamma*, the dynamic stability that planet earth and her related fields like the oceans, atmosphere, stratosphere, and so on will also be affected adversely.

There are numerous Jataka legends relating to how under a righteous ruler, societies prospered in a very friendly and healthy natural environment where people lived in peace and harmony. When kings or rulers became evil, then nature itself rebelled against that nation by creating droughts, floods, earthquakes, civil commotions, and other disasters like communicable and non-communicable diseases. Generally, for good governance, the Buddha taught that kings and rulers should follow the Ten Principles, known as the *dasa raja dhamma*, which are: sharing or beneficence *(dana)*, ethical conduct *(sila)*, recognition and promotion of talent and being charitable to the needy *(pariccada)*, straightforwardness *(ajjava)*, impartiality and composure *(tapan)*, non-hatred *(akrodha)*, non-violence *(avihimsa)*, patience and forgiveness *(kanthi)*, and non-revengefulness *(avirodhitha)*. If we look at present day rulers, how many of them are following the above principles of good governance? In this way, I am not surprised that natural disasters have a relationship to the conduct of humans towards their own kind, towards other creatures and nature, and finally to mother earth.

What we call natural disasters are, therefore, largely human-made. Disasters like droughts, floods, desertification, earth slides, climate change, global warming, melting of icebergs in poles, nuclear accidents, famines, and many communicable and non-communicable diseases such as AIDS, bloody conflicts, violent crimes, and wars are certainly caused by the spiritual degeneration of human society.

Bringing Selfless Spiritual and Religious Teachings Back into Society

At this point, I must explain my views about religion and spirituality. Some educated people are of the view that religion is a personal matter and that it should not be mixed up with social, economic, or political organizations. As a Buddhist I cannot accept this view. On the contrary, I am totally opposed to this narrow perception of religion. In the Noble Eightfold Path, the Buddha advised us of the importance of cultivating Right Views (*samma ditti*), Right Thoughts (*samma sankappa*), Right Words (*samma vaca*), Right Actions (*samma kammanta*), Right Livelihood (*samma ajiva*), Right Effort (*samma vayama*), Right Mindfulness (*samma sati*), and Right Concentration (*samma samadhi*). It is quite clear, even when one has a glance at these eight noble steps, that one has to simultaneously follow these for total self-realization at all times. Buddhists cannot have a dual life or split personality. Both their personal life and public life should work in total harmony so that in their thoughts, words, and deeds, they develop non-greed, non-aversion, and non-egoism.

When we think of cultivating Right Views, Buddha's basic teachings of *anicca* (impermanence), *dukkha* (suffering or unsatisfactoriness), and *anatta* (non-ego) come to one's mind. When we look at the lives we human beings lead, we can always see that what motivates most people throughout their lives is the false views of *nicca* (permanence), *sukha* (comfort), and *atta* (ego). All of human society seems to be absorbed in this ignorance of reality, and hence, when disasters occur, these come to them as totally unexpected incidents. They interfere with their lives that are basically a life-long ego ride towards a permanent and affluent life style they foolishly believe in.

We have in our world a large number of organized religions that people profess. Some of these religions have degenerated themselves, like most other secular organizations, promoting division among human beings and even giving rise to religious wars. If religions are really to be of service to human kind, then they should lead their followers on a path of reduction of their greed for material wealth, power or recognition; their aversion towards other religions, races or communities; and always going on a path of overcoming their egocentricity. In other words religions should work as a means to the spiritual awakening of humanity.

Let us face the true reality of our present way of life. As individuals most of us want to achieve a lifestyle where we can have the maximum gratification of our five senses. The United States, United Kingdom, and European countries for the past five centuries have set the wrong example of the imbalance of material progress compared to spiritual development. Japan and other eastern countries have also followed their wrong example. While we have continued to have our religions in name, in actual fact, besides rituals and outer paraphernalia, we have lost the spiritual content of our religious teachings.

The two most important organs that have the greatest influence on society, namely, political and economic structures, have completely distanced themselves from religious principles. Gradually, social institutions, particularly those related to education, have also dropped spiritual teachings hitherto treated as the most essential component for developing human personalities and also for maintaining justice and peace in society. Even humanitarian disciplines like health have fallen into a materialistic framework, completely destroying thousands of years of healing systems, as well as traditions in agriculture, irrigation, environmental protection, ecological stability, and the protection and use of safe and sustainable energy sources. Today, in all these fields, we are going through crisis after crisis. I am not saying that we should go back to where we were five centuries ago. However, we certainly can have a fresh look at our present problems going beyond economic indicators and the state of stock markets and start thinking anew and taking corrective action.

We are living in the first year of the second decade of the 21st century. We have committed enough blunders in every field of human activity to the extent that we have come to a decisive point. We have to decide whether by a self-centered approach we are going to bring about a destruction of our own societies as well as other nations, or we are going to survive as a human species by being non-selfish.

The Buddha taught us that at the root of all our personal, national, or global problems there are three factors that cause them. They are greed, aversion, and ignorance or delusion. These three evils within our own minds have become so well organized that they bring about all the human made disasters and, I believe, even the natural disasters we are facing at this time. Unless we begin by getting ourselves enlightened to the causes that have brought our human civilization to this critical stage, namely, greed, aversion, and ignorance, we can never hope to be a sustainable and peaceful global society. Why are we subjected to these three evils? It is because we have forgotten to realize the existence of the three fundamental laws of nature; namely, the law of impermanence (*anicca*), the law of suffering (*dukkha*), and the law of non-ego (*anatta*).

A Post 3/11 Vision for Japan: Lessons from Sri Lanka

I think this time—when Japan is trying to resolve the problems caused by the tragedy that took place a few months ago—should be used for an entire re-evaluation of the post Second World War period up to the time of this triple tragedy. In actual fact, not only the government and the people of Japan, but also all governments in the world and global citizens should look back on the past six decades. We all must try to understand not about the successes we achieved but about the failures we encountered that have brought about the present global crisis.

If we look back into the period before Western expansion and the dawn of the industrial age, we find that in spite of all kinds of armed conflicts within and between nations, our societies still remained sustainable as a whole based on community organization and peaceful and mutual cooperative lifestyles. Whatever external improvements we made to make our lives more comfortable, we still paid great importance to personal spiritual awakening by following the principles of a variety of religions. In our part of the world, the teachings of the Buddha influenced our civilizations, one after another. Even today, in spite of all the scientific and technological revolutions that have taken place, the Buddha's teachings remain like a beacon of light to dispel the ignorance we have created. Many scholars point out that the present global crisis is the result of the spiritual and moral decline of the human community. Hence, a transformation of human consciousness should be brought about initially, followed by economic and political transformation.

At present, there is a struggle between violence and non-violence going on in all corners of the globe. Sarvodaya does not believe in violence or terror. It believes in the building of a critical mass of peace consciousness and the cultivation of non-violent and just attitudes within nations and between them. To achieve this, we have to work in three inter-related sectors: consciousness, economics, and power. The transformation of consciousness is a spiritual process; the transformation of economy is a development exercise; and the transformation of power is a political and constitutional matter. In all three sectors, we are working to build a critical mass of transformation in Sri Lanka.

We are helping the poor and powerless to awaken their consciousness, develop their full potential, and build institutions and self-development structures. Sarvodaya aims at encouraging individuals and communities to invest in beneficence. We believe in people's power, supported by the strength of dharma. The dharma that they are trained in ensures they act with clarity of purpose, are mindful of the difficulties of others, and do not harm the environment. This is not a mono-cultural formula for all the ills in the world, yet its followers, by sheer hard work, have released an integrated series of processes.

In each village, a program based on self–reliance, community participation, and a simple plan decided upon by the people themselves has been implemented. From pre-school children, through school going children, youth, mothers, farmers, and other adults, activities are planned and implemented. A village level Sarvodaya Shramadana Society is organized in due course and legally registered with the government. These societies thus have opportunities to engage themselves in economic activities that benefit the village people. The village in its basic needs satisfaction program needs a variety of trained personnel, such as pre-school workers, healthcare workers, nutrition workers, community shop keepers, savings and credit organizers, rural technical service workers, agricultural promoters, and so on. The workers are trained at divisional level, district level, and national level development educational centers. Also the innovative and non-violent power of the people as a whole improves the quality of life in the way they want, strengthened by the process of working together in a variety of fields that affect their lives.

We help the villagers to go through a psychological, social, legal, and economic infrastructure, building phases including a political self-governance phase, all of which begin at the village level. These are based on an alternative life style where simplicity and need based local economies are promoted. Greed based economic pursuits are discouraged. The use of less energy, organic agriculture, protecting the natural fertility of the soil, conservation and protection of natural water sources, and caring for the environment are some of the features of the new way of life that Sarvodaya is promoting.

When a community of people is thus organized, they can become a part of the solution to national and global problems. We first begin with ourselves, to understand our own personality awakening; from infancy, childhood, youth, adulthood, and old age up to the dying moment when we learn to breathe our last with right awareness. A human being who fails to understand the physical, mental, emotional, psychological, and spiritual processes that his or her own personality is going through every moment will never find true happiness and the joy of living in this life. For all above stages of human development, we have scientifically developed practical programs from which thousands of people are daily gaining benefit. No human made divisions among people will interfere with these learning processes, and hence the human consciousness will progressively revert back to its original pure form to realize the highest goal of human evolution: the realization of the truth that all living beings are interconnected and interdependent and that we should live for the well-being of all.

Afterword
The Future of Buddhism in Post 3/11 Japan

Rev. Masazumi Shojun Okano

---

*R**ev. Masazumi Shojun Okano is the President of the Kodo Kyodan Buddhist Fellowship and the Director of the International Buddhist Exchange Center (IBEC), publisher of this volume.*

This volume has been an account of how Japanese Buddhists have responded to what is called in Japan the Great East Japan Earthquake (higashi nihon dai shinsai). The disaster that struck a large part of Eastern Japan on March 11, 2011 has brought so much suffering to a great number of people. As has been pointed out in this volume, the areas that have been damaged by the earthquake, tsunami, and nuclear meltdown had already been suffering from various economic and social problems. The old farming and fishing communities in these regions lost so much of their economic, social, and cultural assets in the process of the great Economic Miracle that characterised the earlier part of post-war Japanese history.

Rapid industrialization and urbanization were the two main factors that drove this country's unprecedented economic development in a short period of time. In 1950, the urban-rural population ratio was 3 to 7. In 1960, the ratio had flipped to 7 to 3. Now more than 80% of Japanese live in urban areas. The large cities during this economic development absorbed an influx of young people from the farming and fishing communities to work in factories and offices. In the process, these communities were left with a large aging population that could no longer support itself economically. The local governments in these areas were thus forced to cut their social welfare budgets, which resulted in closing down many public health and social welfare facilities. In this way, even before the 3/11 disaster, many of these areas did not have enough hospitals. This was part of the reason why many old and sick people died without proper medical care in the weeks after the tsunami.

As explained in this volume, the problems found in the communities where nuclear power plants are located also tell the story of the areas that were left behind during the period of rapid economic development. The large sums of "donations" that were given by TEPCO and the national government were gladly received by the financially challenged local governments in compensation for the "inconveniences" caused by the nuclear power stations. The 3/11 disaster, as we can see, is not only about earthquake, tsunami, and nuclear catastrophe but also about social and economic structural problems inherent in contemporary Japanese society.

These changes in the social and economic structures are in fact partly responsible for the decline of the traditional Buddhist denominations. A very large proportion of traditional Buddhist temples are located in rural areas, and for centuries they were supported by the local inhabitants. Rural areas, however, have been suffering from depopulation, and so the local temples are in serious financial difficulties.

The temples in urban areas also suffer for various reasons. Secularization and institutionalization are two of them. Religious worldviews and religious institutions can no longer exercise the strong influences that they used to hold on wider society. Social conditions and social values have changed, but traditional Buddhist denominations have not been able to respond adequately. Institutionalization that is deeply rooted in the culture of these denominations makes them inwardly-focused and not very attentive to the spiritual and psychological needs of the people. The denominations are seen by people as being unable to respond to these needs that are ever-changing and ever-diversifying, especially in urban areas.

Crisis is sometimes the only remedy for institutionalization. The 3/11 disaster—an unprecedented crisis in recent Japanese history— may work as a catalyst for revitalizing and re-orienting the traditional Buddhist denominations. The accounts in this volume have shown glimpses of that. What will come out of the various aid work that has been carried out by the Buddhist world remains to be seen. However, we can already see the possibilities of change in these denominations through the relief work of their priests. Let us look into this further by examining three groups of actors who have been engaged in aid work.

The first are the priests and their families whose temples are located in the disaster areas. Many of them have shown very strong commitment to the welfare of not only their parishioners but also the general victims in their areas. Noticeable among their various activities was using their temples as shelters for the victims and consoling those who lost their loved ones by voluntarily performing funeral and memorial rites. It is worth pointing out that the attitudes of the mass media have changed to some extent towards the Buddhist priests because of these activities. The mass media especially after the Aum Shinrikyo sarin gas attack in 1995 has repeatedly painted negative pictures of religious organizations. Using various negative stereotypes was the primary way in depicting institutional religion, but there are signs of change seen especially in their reporting of the Buddhist priests' role in caring for disaster victims. Traditional Buddhist funeral rites were described as obsolete and expensive in the pre-3/11 media, but many people have come to realize the power of these rites in helping victims deal with their deep sorrow. Change in the perceptions of the people towards Buddhist priests may in turn change the priests themselves by giving them more confidence in assuming larger social roles. However, more importantly, what is expected of them is their ability to give answers to the question of suffering. The victims want to know why they have to suffer so much. It may be through religious answers to this question that they can find the strength to live through this tremendous hardship. It is therefore important for local priests in the disaster areas to find ways to satisfy these needs of the victims.

The second group of actors are the individual priests who come from outside the disaster areas and have been engaged in various relief work. This group refers to those priests who were not officially sent by their denominations but have chosen on their own to work in and for the disaster areas. Many of them had already been engaged in various forms of social work before 3/11. Some of them have a long history of relief work inside and outside Japan. Thus, they were very quick in responding to the 3/11 disaster. Those priests, although not many in number, are highly organized, and many of them work in cooperation with government organizations, NGOs, and civil society groups. There are also those who are members of inter-denominational groups that deal with social problems such as suicide, poverty, and youth problems. Many of them have been working in the disaster areas by using their expertise in these fields. The priests who are members of the anti-nuclear movement are also part of the second group. They had been engaged mainly in advocacy work in the past, but they have also begun to work for the victims of nuclear contamination in more direct ways by using their expert knowledge. The priests in the second group are the minority in the traditional Buddhist world, but if they can inspire others to work with them or start new groups, they may play a role in changing the traditional denominations.

The third group refers to the denominations themselves and the official inter-denominational bodies such as Japan Buddhist Federation. The administrative bodies of each denomination have come up with budgets for restoring their temples that were destroyed. Many of them have also donated a large amount of money to the Japanese Red Cross Society and other large aid groups. However, in terms of relief work, we have to say that the involvement of central denominational administrative bodies has not been very impressive. Impressive, though, are the activities of the youth associations of some denominations. The National Soto Youth Association, whose activities are introduced in this volume, is one of them. Some others are planning to reinforce their organizations so that they can do better aid work in the future. These youth associations are the bright spots for the denominations' future. When these young priests start occupying higher positions within the denominations in the future, things may change drastically.

Inter-denominational and inter-religious cooperation may be an important factor in changing the inward-looking tendencies of the traditional Buddhist denominations. Inter-denominational exchange and cooperation are seen at different levels. At one level, there are those groups that are formed on a voluntary basis by individual priests who are connected through interests in particular activities, such as suicide prevention work. Regional inter-denominational and inter-religious associations, on the other hand, have a strong presence in some regional areas. In some disaster areas, these associations played important roles morial rites for the victims. The Zenseikyo Foundation & Buddhist Council for Youth and Child Welfare, as mentioned in this volume, is an association of traditional denominations that is formed specifically to deal with youth and child issues. Their administrative office staff has been working in the disaster areas using their expertise in childcare. Although the activities of these inter-denominational associations are meaningful in themselves, their influence over changing the denominations' introverted tendencies is rather limited.

The Japan Buddhist Federation (JBF), on the other hand, may theoretically have a better chance in this matter. JBF aims at forming a basis for an all-encompassing inter-denominational exchange and cooperation in the traditional Buddhist world. It also acts as an interest group that has official communication channels with government bodies and the media. Their activities have mainly centred around information exchange, educational work for members, and compiling official statements and declarations on various issues on behalf of the traditional Buddhist world. JBF, however, has been rather weak on bringing their member denominations together to take concrete action on social issues. Although the JBF's anti-nuclear declaration is a big step forward, it remains to be seen if they can actually mobilize their members to take concerted actions towards achieving the goal.

This volume has been an attempt to describe how the traditional Buddhist world in Japan has responded to the 3/11 disaster. Its accounts are not by any means exhaustive. Women's roles, for example, in the various relief work have not been examined here. There are also many other actors and issues that have been omitted. However, we hope that this book has given an insight into certain realities of the 3/11 disaster and the activities of Buddhists to deal with them.

March 21, 2012
Yokohama, Japan